K-1 PETITION FOR FIANCÉE

Attorney Brian D. Lerner

Law Offices of Brian D. Lerner, A Professional Corporation

Attorney Brian D. Lerner

K-1 Petition for Fiancée

K-1 Petition for Fiancée

Written by Attorney Brian D. Lerner
Copyright © 2021, by Immigration Law Offices of Brian D. Lerner, APC
All rights reserved.

Disclaimer and Terms of Use:

Effort has been made to ensure that the information in this book is accurate and complete. However, the author and the publisher do not warrant that this particular petition will mirror or be exactly as your situation. There has not been any attorney-client agreement created by the purchase of this petition or application. No legal advice has occurred. The cases, regulations and/or statutes cited may change at any time without notice.

Print ISBN: 978-1-948774-90-1
Ebook ISBN: 978-1-948774-89-5

INTRODUCTION

There are a multitude of different immigration petitions and applications. They are complex and full of requirements. Obviously it would be best to hire and immigration attorney to best prepare the petitions and application. However, this can certainly cost thousands of dollars.

The next best option is to get a sample of the petition written by an experienced immigration attorney. The samples cost a fraction what would be charged by an immigration attorney. However, while the reader has to alter, amend and change the parts of the sample petition to reflect their actual situation, it is a fantastic roadmap for them to use. If the reader has purchased the entire petition or application, they will have real live samples of cover letters, forms, declarations, affidavits and the necessary exhibits to use. The samples come from real cases and the names of those clients have been redacted to protect the privacy of that person or corporation.

These are petitions and applications that have been drafted by an experienced immigration attorney with over 25 years of experience. Get the benefits of that experience without the costs.

About the Law Offices of Brian D. Lerner

The Law Offices of Brian D. Lerner, APC. The law practice consists of Immigration and Nationality Law and everything involved with and regarding immigration which includes citizenship, investment visas, family and employment visas, removal and deportation hearings, appeals, waivers, adjustment, consulate processing and all types of immigration and citizenship matters. Thousands of families have been reunited and/or permitted to stay in the U.S. and/or return to the U.S. because of the successful work of Immigration Attorney Brian D. Lerner.

This law offices handles all types of immigration cases including family based and employment based. Immigration issues range from immigration court proceedings to trying to fix what paralegals may have done that was neither correct nor proper. Foreign nationals must have experience lawyers admitted to practice law.

The Law Offices of Brian D. Lerner, APC, handles cases arising from business visas, work permits, Green Cards, non-immigrant visas, deportation, citizenship, appeals and all areas of immigration. The Law Offices of Brian D. Lerner, APC does EB-5 Investor Visas, H-1B Specialty Occupation, L-1 Intracompany Transferee, E-2 Treaty Investor, E-1 Treaty Trader, O-1 Extraordinary Ability among others. Regarding immigrant visas for the Green Card, the firm does PERM and advanced degree PERM, Family Petitions, and Extraordinary Alien Petitions. In addition to affirmative petitions, the Law Firm represents people in deportation and removal hearings, including political asylum, withholding of removal, and convention against torture cases.

Brian D. Lerner has been certified as an expert in Immigration & Nationality Law by the California State Bar, Board of Legal Specialization sicne 2000 and has been re-certified three times. He now passes on his decades of experience by allowing the Reader, Law Schools, Professors and other Immigration Attorneys to purchase sample petitions on every facet of Immigration Law.

TABLE OF CONTENTS

About the K-1 Petition

If you have a fiancée, the last thing you want to do is be separated. However, if you do not do the fiancée petition correctly, that is exactly what will happen. It is not as easy as just showing you're a U.S. Citizen and want to marry someone. Immigration basically thinks you are lying about the validity of the reason you want to get married and are only doing it to get into the U.S. and eventually get the Green Card. You must show the bonafides of the relationship and submit sufficient evidence to show why it would be a real marriage for love. This sample Fiancée Petition is for you. It has everything necessary to give you the best chance possible to get an approval. Just input your own information and use the application as a guide. It has been prepared by an expert Immigration Attorney. Thus, this book will allow you to see a guide of how it is done, prepared and submitted.

SECTION 1
Attorney Cover Letter

Law Offices of Brian D. Lerner

A PROFESSIONAL CORPORATION

CERTIFIED SPECIALIST IN IMMIGRATION AND NATIONALITY LAW
ADMITTED TO THE U.S. SUPREME COURT

LONG BEACH, CALIFORNIA
(562) 495-0554

CARSON, CALIFORNIA
(310) 684-5400

October 1, 2018

USCIS
P.O. Box 660151
Dallas, TX 75266

RE: Petition: I-129F, Petition for Fiancé(e)
        Petitioner: ███████████████
        Beneficiary: ███████████

Dear Sir/Madam:

We hereby submit a K-1 petition on behalf of ███████████████ Petitioner, and ██████
███████ Beneficiary and his fiancee. In support of this petition, we enclose the following documents
for your review:

Form:	Description:
G-1145	E-Notification of Application/Petition Acceptance;
G-28	Notice of Entry of Appearance as Attorney or Accredited Representative (Petitioner);
G-28	Notice of Entry of Appearance as Attorney or Accredited Representative (Beneficiary); and
I-129F	Petition for Alien Fiancé(e) and $535.00 Filing Fee.

We also enclose two (2) passport-style photographs of Petitioner and Applicant.

Exhibits:	Description:
1.	Copy of Birth Certificate of Petitioner;
2.	Copy of Passport of Petitioner;
3.	Copy of Divorce Decree of Petitioner;
4.	Copy of Birth Certificate of Beneficiary;
5.	Copy of Passport of Beneficiary;
6.	Declaration Letter of the Petitioner and the Beneficiary;
7.	Statement to Prove Intention to Marry Within 90 Days of Arrival;
8.	Proof of Communication Between Petitioner and Beneficiary;
9.	Proof that Petitioner and Beneficiary Have Met Each Other in Person;
10.	Copy of Airline Tickets and Itinerary of Petitioner;
11.	Support Letters of Friends and Relative of Petitioner and Beneficiary ;

Pg 2

12.   Copy of Employment Letter of Petitioner;
13.   Copy of Paycheck Stubs of Petitioner;
14.   Copy of 2016-2017 Income Tax Returns and W2 Form of Petitioner; and
15.   Copy of Conviction Records of Petitioner.

I.
INTRODUCTION

Section 101(a)(15)(K) of the Immigration and Nationality Act establishes the requirements for classification as a nonimmigrant fiancé(e) and states as follows:

"(15) The term "immigrant" means every alien except an alien who is within one of the following classes of nonimmigrant aliens."

"(K) An alien who is the fiancé or fiancée of a citizen of the United States and who seeks to enter the United States solely to conclude a valid marriage with the petitioner within ninety days after admission, and the minor children of such fiancé or fiancée accompanying him or following to join him;"

U.S. Citizenship and Immigration Services has interpreted this section of the Act and explained the required procedures and evidence at 8 CFR § 214.2(k), which states as follows in pertinent part:

"(k) Fiancées and fiancés of United States Citizens" Petition and supporting documents. To be classified as a fiancé or fiancée as defined in section 101(a)(15)(K) of the act, an alien must be the beneficiary of an approved visa petition filed on Form I-129F. The petition with supporting documents shall be filed by the petitioner with the director having administrative jurisdiction over the place where the petitioner is residing in the United States. A copy of a document submitted in support of a visa petition filed pursuant to section 214(d) of the act and this paragraph may be accepted, though unaccompanied by the original, if the copy bears a certification by an attorney, typed or rubber-stamped, in the language set forth in §204.2(j) of this chapter. However, the original document shall be submitted if requested by the Service."

II.
PETITIONER IS A U.S. CITIZEN.

In the present case, Petitioner was born in Janesville, Wisconsin and therefore, is a U.S. citizen. See Exhibit 1.

III.
PETITIONER AND BENEFICIARY HAVE MET WITHIN THE LAST TWO YEARS

According to the Code of Federal Regulations, 8 CFR § 214.2(k)(2), there is only one requirement that must be satisfied to demonstrate eligibility for a K-1 visa: the petitioner and the beneficiary must have met within the two years immediately preceding the filing of the instant petition. 8 CFR § 214.2(k)(2) states as follows in pertinent part:

satisfaction of the director that the petitioner and beneficiary have met in person within the two years immediately preceding the filing of the petition." Failure to establish that the petitioner and beneficiary have met within the required period or that compliance with the requirement should be waived shall result in the denial of the petition. Such denial shall be without prejudice to the filing of a new petition once the petitioner and beneficiary have met in person."

Attached please find evidence showing that Petitioner and Beneficiary have met each other in person in Botswana in February 2018. See Exhibit 2,6,9 and 10.

IV.
THIS IS A BONAFIDE RELATIONSHIP.

The evidence herein shows that the relationship is bona fide, have built a relationship and that the relationship was not entered into for purpose of obtaining Lawful Permanent Residency. See Exhibit 8.

V.
THERE IS A BONA FIDE INTENTION TO MARRY WITHIN 90 DAYS OF BENEFICIARY'S ENTRY INTO THE UNITED STATES.

In the present case, as indicated by both Petitioner and Beneficiary, there is a bona fide intention to marry with 90 days of Beneficiary's entry into the United States. See Exhibits 6 and 7.

VI.
CONCLUSION

Based on the foregoing, it is respectfully submitted that all the necessary evidence shows that all the statutory requirements for a fiancée visa have been met and that the instant petition should be approved.

Should you have any further questions, please feel free to contact our office at (562) 495-0554.

Sincerely,

Christopher A. Reed
Attorney at Law

Pg 4

Section 2
Forms

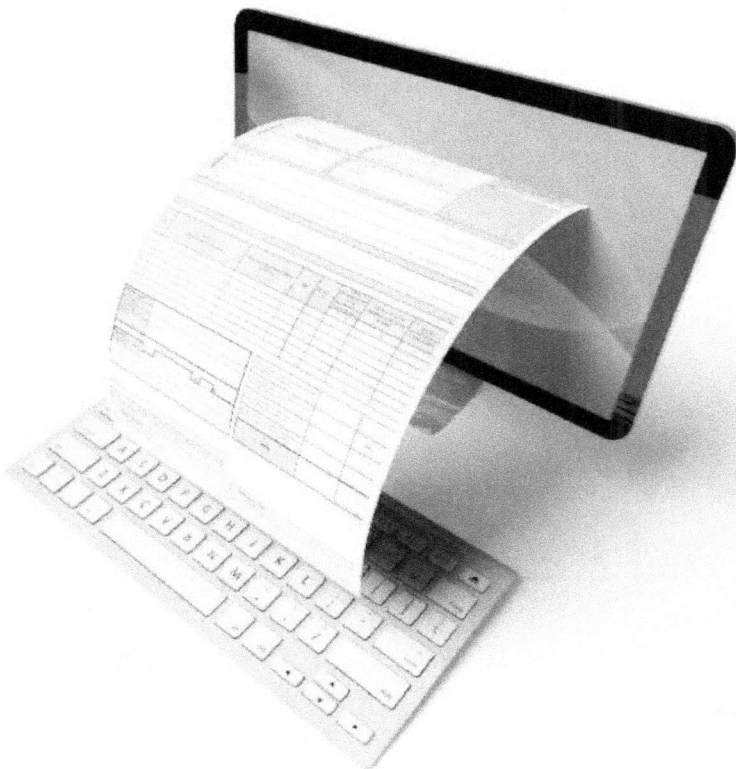

e-Notification of Application/Petition Acceptance

Department of Homeland Security
U.S. Citizenship and Immigration Services

USCIS
Form G-1145

What Is the Purpose of This Form?

Use this form to request an electronic notification (e-Notification) when U.S. Citizenship and Immigration Services accepts your immigration application. This service is available for applications filed at a USCIS Lockbox facility.

General Information

Complete the information below and clip this form to the first page of your application package. You will receive one e-mail and/or text message for each form you are filing.

We will send the e-Notification within 24 hours after we accept your application. Domestic customers will receive an e-mail and/or text message; overseas customers will only receive an e-mail. Undeliverable e-Notifications cannot be resent.

The e-mail or text message will display your receipt number and tell you how to get updated case status information. It will not include any personal information. The e-Notification does not grant any type of status or benefit; rather it is provided as a convenience to customers.

USCIS will also mail you a receipt notice (I-797C), which you will receive within 10 days after your application has been accepted; use this notice as proof of your pending application or petition.

USCIS Privacy Act Statement

AUTHORITIES: The information requested on this form is collected pursuant to section 103(a) of the Immigration and Nationality Act, as amended INA section 101, et seq.

PURPOSE: The primary purpose for providing the information on this form is to request an electronic notification when USCIS accepts immigration form. The information you provide will be used to send you a text and/or email message.

DISCLOSURE: The information you provide is voluntary. However, failure to provide the requested information may prevent USCIS from providing you a text and/or email message receipting your immigration form.

ROUTINE USES: The information provided on this form will be used by and disclosed to DHS personnel and contractors in accordance with approved routine uses, as described in the associated published system of records notices [DHS/USCIS-007 - Benefits Information System and DHS/USCIS-001 - Alien File (A-File) and Central Index System (CIS), which can be found at www.dhs.gov/privacy]. The information may also be made available, as appropriate for law enforcement purposes or in the interest of national security.

Complete this form and clip it on top of the first page of your immigration form(s).

Applicant/Petitioner Full Last Name	Applicant/Petitioner Full First Name	Applicant/Petitioner Full Middle Name
▮	▮	▮

Email Address	Mobile Phone Number (Text Message)
▮gmail.com	562-987-0581

Notice of Entry of Appearance
as Attorney or Accredited Representative

Department of Homeland Security

DHS
Form G-28
OMB No. 1615-0105
Expires 05/31/2021

Part 1. Information About Attorney or Accredited Representative

1. USCIS Online Account Number (if any)

   ▶ [   ]

Name of Attorney or Accredited Representative

2.a. Family Name (Last Name)   **Reed**

2.b. Given Name (First Name)   **Christopher**

2.c. Middle Name   **Allan**

Address of Attorney or Accredited Representative

3.a. Street Number and Name   **3233 E. Broadway**

3.b. ☐ Apt. ☐ Ste. ☐ Flr. [   ]

3.c. City or Town   **Lon gBeach**

3.d. State **CA**   3.e. ZIP Code **90803**

3.f. Province [   ]

3.g. Postal Code [   ]

3.h. Country

   USA

Contact Information of Attorney or Accredited Representative

4. Daytime Telephone Number
   (562) 495-0554

5. Mobile Telephone Number (if any)
   [   ]

6. Email Address (if any)
   creed@eimmigration.org

7. Fax Number (if any)
   (562) 608-8672

Part 2. Eligibility Information for Attorney or Accredited Representative

Select all applicable items.

1.a. ☒ I am an attorney eligible to practice law in, and a member in good standing of, the bar of the highest courts of the following states, possessions, territories, commonwealths, or the District of Columbia. If you need extra space to complete this section, use the space provided in Part 6. Additional Information.

Licensing Authority

   California Supreme Court

1.b. Bar Number (if applicable)

   235438

1.c. I (select only one box) ☒ am not ☐ am subject to any order suspending, enjoining, restraining, disbarring, or otherwise restricting me in the practice of law. If you are subject to any orders, use the space provided in Part 6. Additional Information to provide an explanation.

1.d. Name of Law Firm or Organization (if applicable)

   Law Offices of Brian D. Lerner, APC

2.a. ☐ I am an accredited representative of the following qualified nonprofit religious, charitable, social service, or similar organization established in the United States and recognized by the Department of Justice in accordance with 8 CFR part 1292.

2.b. Name of Recognized Organization
   [   ]

2.c. Date of Accreditation (mm/dd/yyyy)
   [   ]

3. ☐ I am associated with
   [   ],
   the attorney or accredited representative of record who previously filed Form G-28 in this case, and my appearance as an attorney or accredited representative for a limited purpose is at his or her request.

4.a. ☐ I am a law student or law graduate working under the direct supervision of the attorney or accredited representative of record on this form in accordance with the requirements in 8 CFR 292.1(a)(2).

4.b. Name of Law Student or Law Graduate
   [   ]

Form G-28 06/07/19

Part 3. Notice of Appearance as Attorney or Accredited Representative

If you need extra space to complete this section, use the space provided in **Part 6. Additional Information**.

This appearance relates to immigration matters before (select only one box):

1.a. ☒ U.S. Citizenship and Immigration Services (USCIS)

1.b. List the form numbers or specific matter in which appearance is entered.

> **I-129F**

2.a. ☐ U.S. Immigration and Customs Enforcement (ICE)

2.b. List the specific matter in which appearance is entered.

3.a. ☐ U.S. Customs and Border Protection (CBP)

3.b. List the specific matter in which appearance is entered.

4. Receipt Number (if any)
   ▶

5. I enter my appearance as an attorney or accredited representative at the request of the (select **only one** box):

   ☐ Applicant ☒ Petitioner ☐ Requestor
   ☐ Beneficiary/Derivative ☐ Respondent (ICE, CBP)

Information About Client (Applicant, Petitioner, Requestor, Beneficiary or Derivative, Respondent, or Authorized Signatory for an Entity)

6.a. Family Name (Last Name) ▋▋▋▋

6.b. Given Name (First Name) ▋▋▋▋

6.c. Middle Name ▋▋▋▋

7.a. Name of Entity ▋▋ble)

7.b. Title of Authorized Signatory for Entity (if applicable)

8. Client's USCIS Online Account Number (if any)
   ▶

9. Client's Alien Registration Number (A-Number) (if any)
   ▶ A-

Client's Contact Information

10. Daytime Telephone Number
    ▋▋▋▋

11. Mobile Telephone Number (if any)
    ▋▋▋▋

12. Email Address (if any)
    ▋▋▋ **gmail.com**

Mailing Address of Client

NOTE: Provide the client's mailing address. Do not provide the business mailing address of the attorney or accredited representative **unless** it serves as the safe mailing address on the application or petition being filed with this Form G-28.

13.a. Street Number and Name ▋▋▋▋

13.b. ☐ Apt. ☒ Ste. ☐ Flr. **3**

13.c. City or Town ▋▋▋

13.d. State **CA** 13.e. ZIP Code ▋▋▋

13.f. Province

13.g. Postal Code

13.h. Country
> **USA**

Part 4. Client's Consent to Representation and Signature

Consent to Representation and Release of Information

I have requested the representation of and consented to being represented by the attorney or accredited representative named in **Part 1.** of this form. According to the Privacy Act of 1974 and U.S. Department of Homeland Security (DHS) policy, I also consent to the disclosure to the named attorney or accredited representative of any records pertaining to me that appear in any system of records of USCIS, ICE, or CBP.

Part 4. Client's Consent to Representation and Signature (continued)

Options Regarding Receipt of USCIS Notices and Documents

USCIS will send notices to both a represented party (the client) and his, her, or its attorney or accredited representative either through mail or electronic delivery. USCIS will send all secure identity documents and Travel Documents to the client's U.S. mailing address.

If you want to have notices and/or secure identity documents sent to your attorney or accredited representative of record rather than to you, please select **all applicable** items below. You may change these elections through written notice to USCIS.

1.a. [X] I request that USCIS send original notices on an application or petition to the U.S. business address of my attorney or accredited representative as listed in this form.

1.b. [ ] I request that USCIS send any secure identity document (Permanent Resident Card, Employment Authorization Document, or Travel Document) that I receive to the U.S. business address of my attorney or accredited representative (or to a designated military or diplomatic address in a foreign country (if permitted)).

NOTE: If your notice contains Form I-94, Arrival-Departure Record, USCIS will send the notice to the U.S. business address of your attorney or accredited representative. If you would rather have your Form I-94 sent directly to you, select **Item Number 1.c.**

1.c. [ ] I request that USCIS send my notice containing Form I-94 to me at my U.S. mailing address.

Signature of Client or Authorized Signatory for an Entity

2.a. Signature of Client or Authorized Signatory for an Entity

➡ ████████████████████████

2.b. Date of Signature (mm/dd/yyyy) 9/28/2018

Part 5. Signature of Attorney or Accredited Representative

I have read and understand the regulations and conditions contained in 8 CFR 103.2 and 292 governing appearances and representation before DHS. I declare under penalty of perjury under the laws of the United States that the information I have provided on this form is true and correct.

1.a. Signature of Attorney or Accredited Representative

1.b. Date of Signature (mm/dd/yyyy) 10/e/ir

2.a. Signature of Law Student or Law Graduate

2.b. Date of Signature (mm/dd/yyyy)

Form G-28   05/23/18

Part 6. Additional Information

If you need extra space to provide any additional information within this form, use the space below. If you need more space than what is provided, you may make copies of this page to complete and file with this form or attach a separate sheet of paper. Type or print your name at the top of each sheet; indicate the **Page Number**, **Part Number**, and **Item Number** to which your answer refers; and sign and date each sheet.

1.a Family Name
(Last Name)

1.b. Given Name
(First Name)

1.c. Middle Name

2.a. Page Number   2.b. Part Number   2.c. Item Number

2.d.

3.a. Page Number   3.b. Part Number   3.c. Item Number

3.d.

4.a. Page Number   4.b. Part Number   4.c. Item Number

4.d.

5.a. Page Number   5.b. Part Number   5.c. Item Number

5.d.

6.a. Page Number   6.b. Part Number   6.c. Item Number

6.d.

Notice of Entry of Appearance
as Attorney or Accredited Representative

Department of Homeland Security

DHS
Form G-28
OMB No. 1615-0105
Expires 05/31/2021

Part 1. Information About Attorney or Accredited Representative

1. USCIS Online Account Number (if any)

   ▶ [   ]

Name of Attorney or Accredited Representative

2.a. Family Name (Last Name) **Reed**

2.b. Given Name (First Name) **Christopher**

2.c. Middle Name **Allan**

Address of Attorney or Accredited Representative

3.a. Street Number and Name **3233 E. Broadway**

3.b. ☐ Apt. ☐ Ste. ☐ Flr. [   ]

3.c. City or Town **Long Beach**

3.d. State **CA**   3.e. ZIP Code **90803**

3.f. Province **CA**

3.g. Postal Code **90803**

3.h. Country **USA**

Contact Information of Attorney or Accredited Representative

4. Daytime Telephone Number **(562) 495-0554**

5. Mobile Telephone Number (if any) [   ]

6. Email Address (if any) **creed@eimmigration.org**

7. Fax Number (if any) **562) 608-8672**

Part 2. Eligibility Information for Attorney or Accredited Representative

Select all applicable items.

1.a. ☒ I am an attorney eligible to practice law in, and a member in good standing of, the bar of the highest courts of the following states, possessions, territories, commonwealths, or the District of Columbia. If you need extra space to complete this section, use the space provided in Part 6. Additional Information.

   Licensing Authority [   ]

1.b. Bar Number (if applicable) [   ]

1.c. I (select only one box) ☐ am not ☐ am subject to any order suspending, enjoining, restraining, disbarring, or otherwise restricting me in the practice of law. If you are subject to any orders, use the space provided in Part 6. Additional Information to provide an explanation.

1.d. Name of Law Firm or Organization (if applicable) [   ]

2.a. ☐ I am an accredited representative of the following qualified nonprofit religious, charitable, social service, or similar organization established in the United States and recognized by the Department of Justice in accordance with 8 CFR part 1292.

2.b. Name of Recognized Organization [   ]

2.c. Date of Accreditation (mm/dd/yyyy) [   ]

3. ☐ I am associated with [   ]

   the attorney or accredited representative of record who previously filed Form G-28 in this case, and my appearance as an attorney or accredited representative for a limited purpose is at his or her request.

4.a. ☐ I am a law student or law graduate working under the direct supervision of the attorney or accredited representative of record on this form in accordance with the requirements in 8 CFR 292.1(a)(2).

4.b. Name of Law Student or Law Graduate [   ]

Part 3. Notice of Appearance as Attorney or Accredited Representative

If you need extra space to complete this section, use the space provided in **Part 6. Additional Information.**

This appearance relates to immigration matters before (select only one box):

1.a. ☒ U.S. Citizenship and Immigration Services (USCIS)

1.b. List the form numbers or specific matter in which appearance is entered.

> I-129F

2.a. ☐ U.S. Immigration and Customs Enforcement (ICE)

2.b. List the specific matter in which appearance is entered.

3.a. ☐ U.S. Customs and Border Protection (CBP)

3.b. List the specific matter in which appearance is entered.

4. Receipt Number (if any)

▶

5. I enter my appearance as an attorney or accredited representative at the request of the (select only one box):

☒ Applicant ☐ Petitioner ☐ Requestor
☐ Beneficiary/Derivative ☐ Respondent (ICE, CBP)

Information About Client (Applicant, Petitioner, Requestor, Beneficiary or Derivative, Respondent, or Authorized Signatory for an Entity)

6.a. Family Name (Last Name) ▮▮▮▮▮

6.b. Given Name (First Name) ▮▮▮▮▮

6.c. Middle Name

7.a. Name of Entity (if applicable)

7.b. Title of Authorized Signatory for Entity (if applicable)

8. Client's USCIS Online Account Number (if any)

▶

9. Client's Alien Registration Number (A-Number) (if any)

▶ A-

Client's Contact Information

10. Daytime Telephone Number

▮▮▮▮▮

11. Mobile Telephone Number (if any)

▮▮▮▮▮

12. Email Address (if any)

▮▮▮▮▮ gmail.com

Mailing Address of Client

NOTE: Provide the client's mailing address. Do not provide the business mailing address of the attorney or accredited representative unless it serves as the safe mailing address on the application or petition being filed with this Form G-28.

13.a. Street Number and Name   P. O Box 274

13.b. ☐ Apt. ☐ Ste. ☒ Flr.

13.c. City or Town   Tutume

13.d. State   13.e. ZIP Code

13.f. Province

13.g. Postal Code

13.h. Country

> Botswana

Part 4. Client's Consent to Representation and Signature

Consent to Representation and Release of Information

I have requested the representation of and consented to being represented by the attorney or accredited representative named in **Part 1.** of this form. According to the Privacy Act of 1974 and U.S. Department of Homeland Security (DHS) policy, I also consent to the disclosure to the named attorney or accredited representative of any records pertaining to me that appear in any system of records of USCIS, ICE, or CBP.

Part 4. Client's Consent to Representation and Signature (continued)

Options Regarding Receipt of USCIS Notices and Documents

USCIS will send notices to both a represented party (the client) and his, her, or its attorney or accredited representative either through mail or electronic delivery. USCIS will send all secure identity documents and Travel Documents to the client's U.S. mailing address.

If you want to have notices and/or secure identity documents sent to your attorney or accredited representative of record rather than to you, please select **all applicable** items below. You may change these elections through written notice to USCIS.

1.a. ☒ I request that USCIS send original notices on an application or petition to the U.S. business address of my attorney or accredited representative as listed in this form.

1.b. ☐ I request that USCIS send any secure identity document (Permanent Resident Card, Employment Authorization Document, or Travel Document) that I receive to the U.S. business address of my attorney or accredited representative (or to a designated military or diplomatic address in a foreign country (if permitted)).

   NOTE: If your notice contains Form I-94, Arrival-Departure Record, USCIS will send the notice to the U.S. business address of your attorney or accredited representative. If you would rather have your Form I-94 sent directly to you, select **Item Number 1.c.**

1.c. ☐ I request that USCIS send my notice containing Form I-94 to me at my U.S. mailing address.

Signature of Client or Authorized Signatory for an Entity

2.a. Signature of Client or Authorized Signatory for an Entity

➡ [redacted]

2.b. Date of Signature (mm/dd/yyyy)   09/29/2018

Part 5. Signature of Attorney or Accredited Representative

I have read and understand the regulations and conditions contained in 8 CFR 103.2 and 292 governing appearances and representation before DHS. I declare under penalty of perjury under the laws of the United States that the information I have provided on this form is true and correct.

1.a. Signature of Attorney or Accredited Representative

1.b. Date of Signature (mm/dd/yyyy)   10/e/l P

2.a. Signature of Law Student or Law Graduate

2.b. Date of Signature (mm/dd/yyyy)

Part 6. Additional Information

If you need extra space to provide any additional information within this form, use the space below. If you need more space than what is provided, you may make copies of this page to complete and file with this form or attach a separate sheet of paper. Type or print your name at the top of each sheet; indicate the **Page Number**, **Part Number**, and **Item Number** to which your answer refers; and sign and date each sheet.

1.a Family Name
(Last Name)

1.b. Given Name
(First Name)

1.c. Middle Name

2.a. Page Number   2.b. Part Number   2.c. Item Number

2.d.

3.a. Page Number   3.b. Part Number   3.c. Item Number

3.d.

4.a. Page Number   4.b. Part Number   4.c. Item Number

4.d.

5.a. Page Number   5.b. Part Number   5.c. Item Number

5.d.

6.a. Page Number   6.b. Part Number   6.c. Item Number

6.d.

Petition for Alien Fiancé(e)
Department of Homeland Security
U.S. Citizenship and Immigration Services

USCIS
Form I-129F
OMB No. 1615-0001
Expires 08/31/2018

For USCIS Use Only	Fee Stamp	Action Block
Case ID Number		
A-Number		
G-28 Number		

☐ The petition is approved for status under Section 101(a)(15)(K). It is valid for 4 months and expires on:	Extraordinary Circumstances Waiver	
	☐ Approved	Reason
	☐ Denied	

General Waiver		Mandatory Waiver		AMCON: _____
☐ Approved	Reason	☐ Approved	Reason	☐ Personal Interview ☐ Previously Forwarded
☐ Denied		☐ Denied		☐ Document Check ☐ Field Investigation

Initial Receipt	Relocated	Completed	Remarks	IMBRA disclosure to the beneficiary required?
	Received	Approved		☐ Yes ☐ No
Resubmitted	Sent	Returned		

▶ **START HERE - Type or print in black ink.**

Part 1. Information About You

1. Alien Registration Number (A-Number) (if any)
   ▶ A-

2. USCIS Online Account Number (if any)
   ▶

3. U.S. Social Security Number (if any)
   ▶ 3 8 9 8 0 6 8 5 6

Select one box below to indicate the classification you are requesting for your beneficiary:

4.a. ☒ Fiancé(e) (K-1 visa)

4.b. ☐ Spouse (K-3 visa)

5. If you are filing to classify your spouse as a K-3, have you filed Form I-130?   ☐ Yes   ☒ No

Your Full Name

6.a. Family Name (Last Name) ▮▮▮▮▮

6.b. Given Name (First Name) Matthew

6.c. Middle Name Michael

Other Names Used

Provide all other names you have ever used, including aliases, maiden name, and nicknames. If you need extra space to complete this section, use the space provided in **Part 8. Additional Information.**

7.a. Family Name (Last Name)

7.b. Given Name (First Name)

7.c. Middle Name

Your Mailing Address

8.a. In Care Of Name

8.b. Street Number and Name   236 Atlantic Avenue

8.c. ☒ Apt. ☐ Ste. ☐ Flr.   3

8.d. City or Town   Long Beach

8.e. State   CA   8.f. ZIP Code   90802

8.g. Province

8.h. Postal Code

8.i. Country   USA

8.j. Is your current mailing address the same as your physical address?   ☒ Yes   ☐ No

If you answered "No," provide your physical address in Item Numbers 9.a. - 9.h.

Your Address History

Provide your physical addresses for the last five years, whether inside or outside the United States. Provide your current address first if it is different from your mailing address in Item Numbers 8.a. - 8.i. If you need extra space to complete this section, use the space provided in **Part 8. Additional Information.**

Physical Address 1

9.a. Street Number and Name | 236 Atlantic Avenue

9.b. [X] Apt. [ ] Ste. [ ] Flr. | 3

9.c. City or Town | Long Beach

9.d. State | CA   9.e. ZIP Code | 90802

9.f. Province

9.g. Postal Code

9.h. Country | Long Beach

10.a. Date From (mm/dd/yyyy) | 06/01/2015

10.b. Date To (mm/dd/yyyy) | PRESENT

Physical Address 2

11.a. Street Number and Name | 68 Lime Avenue

11.b. [X] Apt. [ ] Ste. [ ] Flr. | 11

11.c. City or Town | Long Beach

11.d. State | CA   11.e. ZIP Code | 90802

11.f. Province

11.g. Postal Code

11.h. Country | USA

12.a. Date From (mm/dd/yyyy) | 03/01/2013

12.b. Date To (mm/dd/yyyy) | 06/01/2015

Your Employment History

Provide your employment history for the last five years, whether inside or outside the United States. Provide your current employment first. If you need extra space to complete this section, use the space provided in **Part 8. Additional Information.**

Employer 1

13. Full Name of Employer
Coast Surveying, Inc.

14.a. Street Number and Name | 15031 Parkway Loop

14.b. [ ] Apt. [X] Ste. [ ] Flr. | B

14.c. City or Town | Tustin

14.d. State | CA   14.e. ZIP Code | 92780

14.f. Province

14.g. Postal Code

14.h. Country | USA

15. Your Occupation (specify)
Party Chief/Land Surveyor

16.a. Employment Start Date (mm/dd/yyyy) | 07/24/2015

16.b. Employment End Date (mm/dd/yyyy) | Present

Employer 2

17. Full Name of Employer
Forkert Engineering and Surveying, Inc.

18.a. Street Number and Name | 22311 Brookhurst Street

18.b. [ ] Apt. [X] Ste. [ ] Flr. | 201

18.c. City or Town | Huntington Beach

18.d. State | CA   18.e. ZIP Code | 92646

18.f. Province

18.g. Postal Code

18.h. Country | USA

19. Your Occupation (specify)
Chainman/Land Surveyor

Part 1. Information About You (continued)

20.a. Employment Start Date (mm/dd/yyyy) — 11/01/2010

20.b. Employment End Date (mm/dd/yyyy) — 07/23/2015

Other Information

21. Gender ☒ Male ☐ Female

22. Date of Birth (mm/dd/yyyy) — 03/17/1976

23. Marital Status
☐ Single ☐ Married ☒ Divorced ☐ Widowed

24. City/Town/Village of Birth
Janesville

25. Province or State of Birth
Wisconsin

26. Country of Birth
USA

Information About Your Parents

Parent 1's Information

27.a. Family Name (Last Name) ███

27.b. Given Name (First Name) ███

27.c. Middle Name ███

28. Date of Birth (mm/dd/yyyy) — 03/02/1949

29. Gender ☒ Male ☐ Female

30. Country of Birth
USA

31.a. City/Town/Village of Residence
Delavan

31.b. Country of Residence
USA

Parent 2's Information

32.a. Family Name (Last Name) — SHIIMER

32.b. Given Name (First Name) — Janet

32.c. Middle Name — Lee

33. Date of Birth (mm/dd/yyyy) — 09/08/1948

34. Gender ☐ Male ☒ Female

35. Country of Birth
USA

36.a. City/Town/Village of Residence
Delavan

36.b. Country of Residence
USA

37. Have you ever been previously married?
☒ Yes ☐ No

If you answered "Yes" to Item Number 37., provide the names of each spouse and the date that each prior marriage ended in Item Numbers 38.a. - 39. If you need extra space to complete this section, use the space provided in Part 8. Additional Information.

Name of Previous Spouse

38.a. Family Name (Last Name) ███

38.b. Given Name (First Name) — Aisha ███

38.c. Middle Name ███

39. Date Marriage Ended (mm/dd/yyyy) — 12/26/2014

Your Citizenship Information

You are a U.S. citizen through (select only one box):

40.a. ☒ Birth in the United States

40.b. ☐ Naturalization

40.c. ☐ U.S. citizen parents

41. Have you obtained a Certificate of Naturalization or a Certificate of Citizenship in your own name?
☐ Yes ☒ No

If you answered "Yes" to Item Number 41., complete Item Numbers 42.a. - 42.c.

Part 1. Information About You (continued)

42.a. Certificate Number

42.b. Place of Issuance

42.c. Date of Issuance (mm/dd/yyyy)

Additional Information

43. Have you ever filed Form I-129F for any other beneficiary? ☐ Yes ☒ No

If you answered "Yes" to Item Number 43., provide the responses to Item Number 44. - 46. for each previous beneficiary. If you need to provide information for more than one beneficiary, use the space provided in **Part 8. Additional Information**.

44. A-Number (if any) ▶ A-

45.a. Family Name (Last Name)

45.b. Given Name (First Name)

45.c. Middle Name

46. Date of Filing (mm/dd/yyyy)

47. What action did USCIS take on Form I-129F (for example, approved, denied, revoked)?

48. Do you have any children under 18 years of age? ☒ Yes ☐ No

If you answered "Yes" to Item Number 48., provide the ages for your children under 18 years of age in Item Numbers 49.a. - 49.b.

Provide the ages for your children under 18 years of age. If you need extra space to complete this section, use the space provided in **Part 8. Additional Information**.

49.a. Age ▉

49.b. Age ▉

Provide all U.S. states and foreign countries in which you have resided since your 18th birthday.

Residence 1

50.a. State **TX**

50.b. Country
USA

Residence 2

51.a. State **CA**

51.b. Country
USA

Part 2. Information About Your Beneficiary

1.a. Family Name (Last Name) ▉

1.b. Given Name (First Name) ▉

1.c. Middle Name

2. A-Number (if any)
▶ A-

3. U.S. Social Security Number (if any)
▶

4. Date of Birth (mm/dd/yyyy) **06/13/1989**

5. Gender ☐ Male ☒ Female

6. Marital Status
☒ Single ☐ Married ☐ Divorced ☐ Widowed

7. City/Town/Village of Birth
Selebi Phikwe

8. Country of Birth
Botswana

9. Country of Citizenship or Nationality
Botswana

Other Names Used

Provide all other names you have ever used, including aliases, maiden name, and nicknames. If you need extra space to complete this section, use the space provided in **Part 8. Additional Information**.

10.a. Family Name (Last Name)

10.b. Given Name (First Name)

10.c. Middle Name

Part 2. Information About Your Beneficiary (continued)

Mailing Address for Your Beneficiary

11.a. In Care Of Name

[redacted]

11.b. Street Number and Name   P.O. Box 274

11.c. ☐ Apt. ☐ Ste. ☐ Flr.

11.d. City or Town   Tutume

11.e. State ___   11.f. ZIP Code ___

11.g. Province   Central

11.h. Postal Code ___

11.i. Country   Botswana

Your Beneficiary's Address History

Provide your beneficiary's physical addresses for the last five years, whether inside or outside the United States. Provide your beneficiary's current address first if it is different from the mailing address in Item Numbers 11.a. - 11.i. If you need extra space to complete this section, use the space provided in Part 8. Additional Information.

Beneficiary's Physical Address 1

12.a. Street Number and Name   Block 1 Plot 1051

12.b. ☐ Apt. ☐ Ste. ☐ Flr.

12.c. City or Town   Mmopane

12.d. State ___   12.e. ZIP Code ___

12.f. Province   Kweneng District

12.g. Postal Code ___

12.h. Country   Botswana

13.a. Date From (mm/dd/yyyy)   12/01/2017

13.b. Date To (mm/dd/yyyy)   PRESENT

Beneficiary's Physical Address 2

14.a. Street Number and Name   [redacted]

14.b. ☐ Apt. ☐ Ste. ☐ Flr.

14.c. City or Town   [redacted]

14.d. State ___   ZIP ___

14.f. Province   Kweneng District

14.g. Postal Code ___

14.h. Country   Botswana

15.a. Date From (mm/dd/yyyy)   03/01/2010

15.b. Date To (mm/dd/yyyy)   12/01/2017

Your Beneficiary's Employment History

Provide your employment history for the last five years, whether inside or outside the United States. Provide your current employment first. If you need extra space to complete this section, use the space provided in Part 8. Additional Information.

Beneficiary's Employer 1

16. Full Name of Employer

[redacted]

17.a. Street Number and Name   [redacted]

17.b. ☐ Apt. ☐ Ste. ☐ Flr.

17.c. City or Town   Gaborone

17.d. State ___   17.e. ZIP Code ___

17.f. Province ___

17.g. Postal Code ___

17.h. Country   Botswana

18. Beneficiary's Occupation (specify)

[redacted]

19.a. Employment Start Date (mm/dd/yyyy)   11/01/2017

19.b. Employment End Date (mm/dd/yyyy)   Present

Part 2. Information About Your Beneficiary (continued)

Beneficiary's Employer 2

20. Full Name of Employer

████████████████

21.a. Street Number and Name   Private Bag 001

21.b. ☐ Apt. ☐ Ste. ☐ Flr. [ ]

21.c. City or Town   Molepolole

21.d. State [ ]   21.e. ZIP Code [ ]

21.f. Province [ ]

21.g. Postal Code [ ]

21.h. Country   Botswana

22. Beneficiary's Occupation (specify)

Nurse

23.a. Employment Start Date (mm/dd/yyyy)   08/01/2012

23.b. Employment End Date (mm/dd/yyyy)   11/0 1/2017

Information About Your Beneficiary's Parents

Parent 1's Information

24.a. Family Name (Last Name)   ████████

24.b. Given Name (First Name)   ████████

24.c. Middle Name [ ]

25. Date of Birth (mm/dd/yyyy)   02/02/1945

26. Gender   ☒ Male   ☐ Female

27. Country of Birth

Botswana

28.a. City/Town/Village of Residence

Tutume

28.b. Country of Residence

Botswana

Parent 2's Information

29.a. Family Name (Last Name)   ████████

29.b. Given Name (First Name)   ████████

29.c. Middle Name [ ]

30. Date of Birth (mm/dd/yyyy)   02/02/1947

31. Gender   ☐ Male   ☒ Female

32. Country of Birth

Botswana

33.a. City/Town/Village of Residence

Tutume

33.b. Country of Residence

Botswana

Other Information About Your Beneficiary

34. Has your beneficiary ever been previously married?   ☐ Yes   ☒ No

If you answered "Yes" to Item Number 34., provide the names of each prior spouse and the date each prior marriage ended in **Item Numbers 35.a. - 36.** If you need to provide information for more than one spouse, use the space provided in **Part 8. Additional Information.**

Name of Previous Spouse

35.a. Family Name (Last Name) [ ]

35.b. Given Name (First Name) [ ]

35.c. Middle Name [ ]

36. Date Marriage Ended (mm/dd/yyyy) [ ]

37. Has your beneficiary ever been in the United States?   ☐ Yes   ☒ No

If your beneficiary is currently in the United States, complete Item Numbers 38.a. - 38.h.

38.a. He or she last entered as a (for example, visitor, student, exchange alien, crewman, stowaway, temporary worker, without inspection):

[ ]

38.b. I-94 Arrival-Departure Record Number   ▶ [ ]

38.c. Date of Arrival (mm/dd/yyyy) [ ]

Part 2. Information About Your Beneficiary (continued)

38.d. Date authorized stay expired or will expire as shown on Form I-94 or I-95 (mm/dd/yyyy)

38.e. Passport Number

38.f. Travel Document Number

38.g. Country of Issuance for Passport or Travel Document

38.h. Expiration Date for Passport or Travel Document (mm/dd/yyyy)

39. Does your beneficiary have any children?
☒ Yes ☐ No

If you answered "Yes" to Item Number 39., provide the following information about each child. If you need to provide information for more than one child, use the space provided in **Part 8. Additional Information.**

Children of Beneficiary

40.a. Family Name (Last Name) ▮▮▮▮

40.b. Given Name (First Name) ▮▮▮▮

40.c. Middle Name ▮▮▮▮

41. Country of Birth
Botswana

42. Date of Birth (mm/dd/yyyy) 12/17/2010

43. Does this child reside with your beneficiary?
☒ Yes ☐ No

If the child does not reside with your beneficiary, provide the child's physical residence.

44.a. Street Number and Name

44.b. ☐ Apt. ☐ Ste. ☐ Flr.

44.c. City or Town

44.d. State ____ **44.e.** ZIP Code

44.f. Province

44.g. Postal Code

44.h. Country

Address in the United States Where Your Beneficiary Intends to Live

45.a. Street Number and Name ▮▮▮▮

45.b. ☒ Apt. ☐ Ste. ☐ Flr. ▮▮▮▮

45.c. City or Town Long Beach

45.d. State CA **45.e.** ZIP Code 90802

46. Daytime Telephone Number ▮▮▮▮

Your Beneficiary's Physical Address Abroad

47.a. Street Number and Name Block 1 Plot 1051

47.b. ☐ Apt. ☐ Ste. ☐ Flr.

47.c. City or Town Mmopane

47.d. Province

47.e. Postal Code

47.f. Country Botswana

48. Daytime Telephone Number ▮▮▮▮

Your Beneficiary's Name and Address in His or Her Native Alphabet

49.a. Family Name (Last Name)

49.b. Given Name (First Name)

49.c. Middle Name

50.a. Street Number and Name

50.b. ☐ Apt. ☐ Ste. ☐ Flr.

50.c. City or Town

50.d. Province

50.e. Postal Code

50.f. Country

Part 2. Information About Your Beneficiary (continued)

51. Is your fiancé(e) related to you?

    ☐ Yes ☒ No ☐ N/A, beneficiary is my spouse

52. Provide the nature and degree of relationship (for example, third cousin or maternal uncle).

    [ ]

53. Have you and your fiancé(e) met in person during the two years immediately before filing this petition?

    ☒ Yes ☐ No ☐ N/A, beneficiary is my spouse

If you answered "Yes" to Item Number 53., describe the circumstances of your in-person meeting in Item Number 54. Attach evidence to demonstrate that you were in each other's physical presence during the required two year period.

If you answered "No," explain your reasons for requesting an exemption from the in person meeting requirement in Item Number 54. and provide evidence that you should be exempt from this requirement. Refer to Part 2., Item Numbers 53. - 54. of the Specific Instructions section of the Instructions for additional information about the requirement to meet. If you need extra space to complete this section, use the space provided in Part 8. Additional Information.

54. **See Attached**

International Marriage Broker (IMB) Information

55. Did you meet your beneficiary through the services of an IMB? ☐ Yes ☒ No

If you answered "Yes" to Item Number 55., provide the IMB's contact information and Website information below. In addition, attach a copy of the signed, written consent form the IMB obtained from your beneficiary authorizing your beneficiary's personal contact information to be released to you.

56. IMB's Name (if any)

    [ ]

57.a. Family Name of IMB (Last Name)

    [ ]

57.b. Given Name of IMB (First Name)

    [ ]

58. Organization Name of IMB

    [ ]

59. Website of IMB

    [ ]

60.a. Street Number and Name [ ]

60.b. ☐ Apt. ☐ Ste. ☐ Flr. [ ]

60.c. City or Town [ ]

60.d. Province [ ]

60.e. Postal Code [ ]

60.f. Country [ ]

61. Daytime Telephone Number

    [ ]

Consular Processing Information

Your beneficiary will apply for a visa abroad at the U.S. Embassy or U.S. Consulate at:

62.a. City or Town

    Gabarone

62.b. Country

    Botswana

Part 3. Other Information

Criminal Information

NOTE: These criminal information questions must be answered even if your records were sealed, cleared, or if anyone, including a judge, law enforcement officer, or attorney, told you that you no longer have a record. If you need extra space to complete this section, use the space provided in Part 8. Additional Information.

1. Have you EVER been subject to a temporary or permanent protection or restraining order (either civil or criminal)? ☒ Yes ☐ No

Have you EVER been arrested or convicted of any of the following crimes:

2.a. Domestic violence, sexual assault, child abuse, child neglect, dating violence, elder abuse, stalking or an attempt to commit any of these crimes? (See Part 3. Other Information, Item Numbers 1. - 3.c. of the Instructions for the full definition of the term "domestic violence.") ☒ Yes ☐ No

Part 3. Other Information (continued)

2.b. Homicide, murder, manslaughter, rape, abusive sexual contact, sexual exploitation, incest, torture, trafficking, peonage, holding hostage, involuntary servitude, slave trade, kidnapping, abduction, unlawful criminal restraint, false imprisonment, or an attempt to commit any of these crimes? ☐ Yes ☒ No

2.c. Three or more arrests or convictions, not from a single act, for crimes relating to a controlled substance or alcohol? ☐ Yes ☒ No

NOTE: If you were ever arrested or convicted of any of the specified crimes, you must submit certified copies of all court and police records showing the charges and disposition for every arrest or conviction. You must do so even if your records were sealed, expunged, or otherwise cleared, and regardless of whether anyone, including a judge, law enforcement officer, or attorney, informed you that you no longer have a criminal record. If you need extra space to complete this section, use the space provided in **Part 8. Additional Information.**

If you have provided information about a conviction for a crime listed in **Item Numbers 2.a. - 2.c.** and you were being battered or subjected to extreme cruelty at the time of your conviction, select all of the following that apply to you:

3.a. ☐ I was acting in self-defense.

3.b. ☐ I violated a protection order issued for my own protection.

3.c. ☐ I committed, was arrested for, was convicted of, or pled guilty to a crime that did not result in serious bodily injury and there was a connection between the crime and me having been battered or subjected to extreme cruelty.

4.a. Have you ever been arrested, cited, charged, indicted, convicted, fined, or imprisoned for breaking or violating any law or ordinance in any country, excluding traffic violations (unless a traffic violation was alcohol- or drug-related or involved a fine of $500 or more)? ☒ Yes ☐ No

4.b. If the answer to **Item Number 4.a.** is "Yes," provide information about each of those arrests, citations, charges, indictments, convictions, fines, or imprisonments in the space below. If you were the subject of an order of protection or restraining order and believe you are the victim, please explain those circumstances and provide any evidence to support your claims. Include the dates and outcomes. If you need extra space to complete this section, use the space provided in **Part 8. Additional Information.**

Multiple Filer Waiver Request Information

Refer to **Part 3. Types of Waivers** in the **Specific Instructions** section of the Instructions for an explanation of the filing waivers.

Indicate which one of the following waivers you are requesting:

5.a. ☐ Multiple Filer, No Permanent Restraining Orders or Convictions for a Specified Offense (**General Waiver**)

5.b. ☐ Multiple Filer, Prior Permanent Restraining Orders or Criminal Conviction for Specified Offense (**Extraordinary Circumstances Waiver**)

5.c. ☐ Multiple Filer, Prior Permanent Restraining Order or Criminal Convictions for Specified Offense Resulting from Domestic Violence (**Mandatory Waiver**)

5.d. ☒ Not applicable, beneficiary is my spouse or I am not a multiple filer

Part 4. Biographic Information

1. Ethnicity (Select only one box)
☐ Hispanic or Latino
☒ Not Hispanic or Latino

2. Race (Select all applicable boxes)
☒ White
☐ Asian
☐ Black or African American
☐ American Indian or Alaska Native
☐ Native Hawaiian or Other Pacific Islander

3. Height   Feet 5   Inches 9

4. Weight   Pounds 1 7 5

5. Eye Color (Select only one box)
☐ Black   ☐ Blue   ☒ Brown
☐ Gray   ☐ Green   ☐ Hazel
☐ Maroon   ☐ Pink   ☐ Unknown/Other

6. Hair Color (Select only one box)
☐ Bald (No hair)   ☐ Black   ☐ Blond
☒ Brown   ☐ Gray   ☐ Red
☐ Sandy   ☐ White   ☐ Unknown/Other

Part 5. Petitioner's Statement, Contact Information, Declaration, and Signature

NOTE: Read the **Penalties** section of the Form I-129F Instructions before completing this part.

Petitioner's Statement

NOTE: Select the box for either **Item Number 1.a.** or **1.b.** If applicable, select the box for **Item Number 2.**

1.a. ☒ I can read and understand English, and I have read and understand every question and instruction on this petition and my answer to every question.

1.b. ☐ The interpreter named in **Part 6.** read to me every question and instruction on this petition and my answer to every question in

a language in which I am fluent, and I understood everything.

2. ☒ At my request, the preparer named in **Part 7.**,

Christopher A. Reed

prepared this petition for me based only upon information I provided or authorized.

Petitioner's Contact Information

3. Petitioner's Daytime Telephone Number

4. Petitioner's Mobile Telephone Number (if any)

5. ▮▮▮▮▮▮▮▮ f any)

Petitioner's Declaration and Certification

Copies of any documents I have submitted are exact photocopies of unaltered, original documents, and I understand that USCIS may require that I submit original documents to USCIS at a later date. Furthermore, I authorize the release of any information from any of my records that USCIS may need to determine my eligibility for the immigration benefit I seek.

I further authorize release of information contained in this petition, in supporting documents, and in my USCIS records to other entities and persons where necessary for the administration and enforcement of U.S. immigration laws.

I understand that USCIS may require me to appear for an appointment to take my biometrics (fingerprints, photograph, and/or signature) and, at that time, if I am required to provide biometrics, I will be required to sign an oath reaffirming that:

1) I provided or authorized all of the information contained in, and submitted with, my petition;

2) I reviewed and understood all of the information in, and submitted with, my petition; and

3) All of this information was complete, true, and correct at the time of filing.

I certify, under penalty of perjury, that all of the information in my petition and any document submitted with it were provided or authorized by me, that I reviewed and understand all of the information contained in, and submitted with, my petition, and that all of this information is complete, true, and correct.

Petitioner's Signature

6.a. ▮▮▮▮▮▮▮▮▮▮▮▮ ink)

6.b. Date of Signature (mm/dd/yyyy) | 9/28/2018

NOTE TO ALL PETITIONERS: If you do not completely fill out this petition or fail to submit required documents listed in the Instructions, USCIS may deny your petition.

Part 6. Interpreter's Contact Information, Certification, and Signature

Provide the following information about the interpreter.

Interpreter's Full Name

1.a. Interpreter's Family Name (Last Name)

1.b. Interpreter's Given Name (First Name)

2. Interpreter's Business or Organization Name (if any)

Interpreter's Mailing Address

3.a. Street Number and Name

3.b. ☐ Apt. ☐ Ste. ☐ Flr.

3.c. City or Town

3.d. State

3.e. ZIP Code

3.f. Province

3.g. Postal Code

3.h. Country

Pg 24

Part 6. Interpreter's Contact Information, Certification, and Signature (continued)

Interpreter's Contact Information

4. Interpreter's Daytime Telephone Number

5. Interpreter's Mobile Telephone Number (if any)

6. Interpreter's Email Address (if any)

Interpreter's Certification

I certify, under penalty of perjury, that:

I am fluent in English and [   ]
which is the same language specified in **Part 5., Item Number 1.b.**, and I have read to this petitioner in the identified language every question and instruction on this petition and his or her answer to every question. The petitioner informed me that he or she understands every instruction, question, and answer on the petition, including the **Petitioner's Declaration and Certification**, and has verified the accuracy of every answer.

Interpreter's Signature

7.a. Interpreter's Signature (sign in ink)

7.b. Date of Signature (mm/dd/yyyy)

Part 7. Contact Information, Declaration, and Signature of the Person Preparing this Petition, if Other Than the Petitioner

Provide the following information about the preparer.

Preparer's Full Name

1.a. Preparer's Family Name (Last Name)

Reed

1.b. Preparer's Given Name (First Name)

Christopher

2. Preparer's Business or Organization Name (if any)

Law Offices of Brian D. Lerner, APC

Preparer's Mailing Address

3.a. Street Number and Name 3233 E. Broadway

3.b. ☐ Apt. ☐ Ste. ☐ Flr. [   ]

3.c. City or Town Long Beach

3.d. State CA   3.e. ZIP Code 90803

3.f. Province

3.g. Postal Code

3.h. Country

USA

Preparer's Contact Information

4. Preparer's Daytime Telephone Number

(562) 495-0554

5. Preparer's Mobile Telephone Number (if any)

6. Preparer's Email Address (if any)

creed@eimmigration.org

Preparer's Statement

7.a. ☐ I am not an attorney or accredited representative but have prepared this petition on behalf of the petitioner and with the petitioner's consent.

7.b. ☒ I am an attorney or accredited representative and my representation of the petitioner in this case ☒ extends ☐ does not extend beyond the preparation of this petition.

NOTE: If you are an attorney or accredited representative whose representation extends beyond preparation of this petition, you may be obliged to submit a completed Form G-28, Notice of Entry of Appearance as Attorney or Accredited Representative, or G-28I, Notice of Entry of Appearance as Attorney In Matters Outside the Geographical Confines of the United States, with this petition.

Pg 25

Part 7. Contact Information, Declaration, and Signature of the Person Preparing this Petition, if Other Than the Petitioner (continued)

Preparer's Certification

By my signature, I certify, under penalty of perjury, that I prepared this petition at the request of the petitioner. The petitioner then reviewed this completed petition and informed me that he or she understands all of the information contained in, and submitted with, his or her petition, including the **Petitioner's Declaration and Certification**, and that all of this information is complete, true, and correct. I completed this petition based only on information that the petitioner provided to me or authorized me to obtain or use.

Preparer's Signature

8.a. Preparer's Signature (sign in ink)

8.b. Date of Signature (mm/dd/yyyy)   10/2/1?

Part 8. Additional Information

If you need extra space to provide any additional information within this petition, use the space below. If you need more space than what is provided, you may make copies of this page to complete and file with this petition or attach a separate sheet of paper. Type or print your name and A-Number (if any) at the top of each sheet; indicate the **Page Number**, **Part Number**, and **Item Number** to which your answer refers; and sign and date each sheet.

1.a Family Name
    (Last Name) ▮▮▮▮▮

1.b. Given Name
     (First Name) ▮▮▮▮▮

1.c. Middle Name | Michael

2.   A-Number (if any) ▶ A-

3.a. Page Number | 4
3.b. Part Number | 1
3.c. Item Number

3.d.
50.a. - WI
50.b. - USA

4.a. Page Number
4.b. Part Number
4.c. Item Number
4.d.

5.a. Page Number
5.b. Part Number
5.c. Item Number
5.d.

6.a. Page Number
6.b. Part Number
6.c. Item Number
6.d.

7.a. Page Number
7.b. Part Number
7.c. Item Number
7.d.

████████ ██████ Form: I-129F (Page 1)

Part 2 40. Additional Children of Beneficiary:
Relationship: Child
Family Name ██████ ; Given Name: Sesame ; Date of Birth: 09/30/2014;

SECTION 3

EXHIBITS

Exhibit 1

Copy of Birth Certificate of Petitioner

WISCONSIN CERTIFICATE OF VITAL RECORD

ORIGINAL CERTIFICATE OF LIVE BIRTH

STATE FILE NUMBER: ▮▮▮▮

LEGACY STATE FILE NUMBER: ▮▮▮▮

FILE DATE: MARCH 30, 1976

Child's Name: First	Middle	Last
▮▮▮▮	MICHAEL	▮▮▮▮

Sex:	Date of Birth:	Facility Name:	Birth Occurred Inside City, Village, Township:	County of Birth:
MALE	MARCH 17, 1976	MERCY HOSPITAL	JANESVILLE	ROCK

Time of Birth:	Birthweight:	Plurality:
03:51 AM	7 lbs 15 oz	Single

Mother's Birth Name: First	Middle	Last
JANET	LEE	▮▮▮▮

Mother's Place of Birth:	Mother's Age:
ILLINOIS	27

Mother's Residence - City, Village, TWP:	Residence - County:	Residence - State:
DELAVAN	ROCK	WISCONSIN

Father's Birth Name: First	Middle	Last
WILLIAM	LELAND	▮▮▮▮

Father's Place of Birth:	Father's Age:
ILLINOIS	27

REGISTER OF DEEDS
ROCK CO.
LOCAL REGISTRAR

I certify that this document contains a true and correct reproduction of facts on file with the Wisconsin Vital Records Office.

STATE OF

Exhibit 2

Copy of Passport of Petitioner;

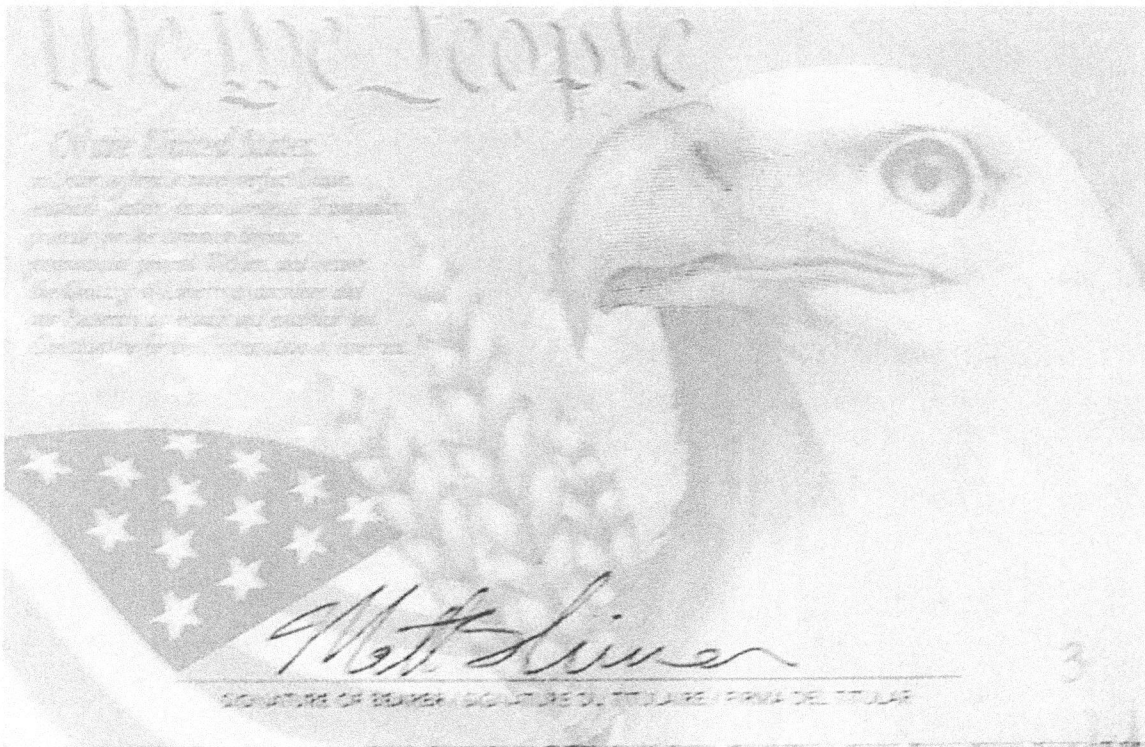

PASSPORT
PASSEPORT
PASAPORTE

U.S.A.

UNITED STATES OF AMERICA

P   USA   569009075

Nationality / Nationalité / Nacionalidad
UNITED STATES OF AMERICA

Date of birth / Date de naissance / Fecha de nacimiento
17 Mar 1976

Place of birth / Lieu de naissance / Lugar de nacimiento
WISCONSIN, U.S.A.

Date of issue / Date de délivrance / Fecha de expedición
13 Oct 2017

Date of expiration / Date d'expiration / Fecha de caducidad
12 Oct 2027

Sex / Sexe / Sexo
M

Authority / Autorité / Autoridad
United States
Department of State

Endorsements / Mentions Spéciales / Anotaciones
SEE PAGE 27

USA

Pg 33

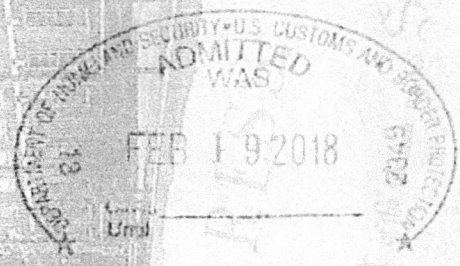

Visas

"Let us raise a standard to which the wise and honest can repair"
George Washington

Visas

Exhibit 3

Copy of Divorce Decree of Petitioner;

ATTORNEY OR PARTY WITHOUT ATTORNEY (Name, State bar number, and address)	FOR COURT USE ONLY

▊ M. ▊
68 LIME AVE #11
LONG BEACH, CA 90802
TELEPHONE NO: (562) 987-0581   FAX NO (Optional)
E-MAIL ADDRESS (Optional)
ATTORNEY FOR (Name)   IN PRO PER

SUPERIOR COURT OF CALIFORNIA, COUNTY OF   LOS ANGELES
STREET ADDRESS 110 NORTH GRAND AVE
MAILING ADDRESS 110 NORTH GRAND AVE
CITY AND ZIP CODE LOS ANGELES, CA 90012
BRANCH NAME CENTRAL

PETITIONER ▊ M. ▊

RESPONDENT ▊

FOR COURT USE ONLY

CONFORMED COPY
ORIGINAL FILED
Superior Court of California
County of Los Angeles

DEC 2 6 2014

Sherri R. Carter, Executive Officer/Clerk
By: Michelle Zarate, Deputy

NOTICE OF ENTRY OF JUDGMENT	CASE NUMBER ▊

HON. MICHELLE WILLIAMS COURT, DEPT. 67

You are notified that the following judgment was entered on (date):

1. [X] Dissolution
2. [ ] Dissolution - status only
3. [ ] Dissolution - reserving jurisdiction over termination of marital status or domestic partnership
4. [ ] Legal separation
5. [ ] Nullity
6. [ ] Parent-child relationship
7. [ ] Judgment on reserved issues
8. [ ] Other (specify):

Date:

Clerk, by _____, Deputy

-NOTICE TO ATTORNEY OF RECORD OR PARTY WITHOUT ATTORNEY-

Under the provisions of Code of Civil Procedure section 1952, if no appeal is filed the court may order the exhibits destroyed or otherwise disposed of after 60 days from the expiration of the appeal time.

STATEMENT IN THIS BOX APPLIES ONLY TO JUDGMENT OF DISSOLUTION
Effective date of termination of marital or domestic partnership status (specify):
WARNING: Neither party may remarry or enter into a new domestic partnership until the effective date of the termination of marital or domestic partnership status, as shown in this box.

CLERK'S CERTIFICATE OF MAILING

I certify that I am not a party to this cause and that a true copy of the Notice of Entry of Judgment was mailed first class, postage fully prepaid, in a sealed envelope addressed as shown below, and that the notice was mailed

at (place): LOS ANGELES   , California, on (date)

Date: Clerk, by _____, Deputy

— Name and address of petitioner or petitioner's attorney —	— Name and address of respondent or respondent's attorney —
▊ M. ▊ 68 LIME AVE #11 LONG BEACH, CA 90802	▊ N6637 COUNTY RD O ELKHORN, WI 53121

Page 1 of 1

Form Adopted
Judicial
FL-190 [I]

5, 7637
ca.gov

ATTORNEY OR PARTY WITHOUT ATTORNEY (Name, State Bar number, and address):

████ M. ████████
68 LIME AVE #11
LONG BEACH, CA 90802
TELEPHONE NO. (562)987-0581   FAX NO. (Optional):
E-MAIL ADDRESS (Optional):
ATTORNEY FOR (name): IN PRO PER

SUPERIOR COURT OF CALIFORNIA, COUNTY OF LOS ANGELES
STREET ADDRESS: 110 NORTH GRAND AVE
MAILING ADDRESS: 110 NORTH GRAND AVE
CITY AND ZIP CODE: LOS ANGELES, CA 90012
BRANCH NAME: CENTRAL

FOR COURT USE ONLY

CONFORMED COPY
ORIGINAL FILED
Superior Court of California
County of Los Angeles

DEC 26 2014

Sherri R. Carter, Executive Officer/Clerk
By: Michelle Zarate, Deputy

MARRIAGE OR PARTNERSHIP OF
PETITIONER: ████ M. ████████
RESPONDENT: ████ ████████

JUDGMENT

[X] DISSOLUTION   [ ] LEGAL SEPARATION   [ ] NULLITY
  [ ] Status only
  [ ] Reserving jurisdiction over termination of marital or domestic partnership status
  [ ] Judgment on reserved issues
Date marital or domestic partnership status ends:

CASE NUMBER
████████

HON. MICHELLE WILLIAMS COURT, DEPT. 67

1. [ ] This judgment [ ] contains personal conduct restraining orders [ ] modifies existing restraining orders
   The restraining orders are contained on page(s) _____ of the attachment. They expire on (date).

2. This proceeding was heard as follows: [X] Default or uncontested [X] By declaration under Family Code section 2336
   [ ] Contested   [ ] Agreement in court
   a. Date: _____ Dept.: X _____ Room: _____
   b. Judicial officer (name): MARK A. JUHAS, JUDGE   [ ] Temporary judge
   c. [ ] Petitioner present in court   [ ] Attorney present in court (name):
   d. [ ] Respondent present in court   [ ] Attorney present in court (name):
   e. [ ] Claimant present in court (name):   [ ] Attorney present in court (name):
   f. [ ] Other (specify name):

3. The court acquired jurisdiction of the respondent on (date): 12/17/2013
   a. [X] The respondent was served with process.
   b. [ ] The respondent appeared.

THE COURT ORDERS, GOOD CAUSE APPEARING

4. a. [X] Judgment of dissolution is entered. Marital or domestic partnership status is terminated and the parties are restored to the status of single persons
      (1) [X] on (specify date):
      (2) [ ] on a date to be determined on noticed motion of either party or on stipulation
   b. [ ] Judgment of legal separation is entered.
   c. [ ] Judgment of nullity is entered. The parties are declared to be single persons on the ground of (specify).

   d. [ ] This judgment will be entered nunc pro tunc as of (date):
   e. [ ] Judgment on reserved issues.
   f. The [ ] petitioner's [ ] respondent's former name is restored to (specify):
   g. [ ] Jurisdiction is reserved over all other issues, and all present orders remain in effect except as provided below.
   h. [ ] This judgment contains provisions for child support or family support. Each party must complete and file with the court a Child Support Case Registry Form (form FL-191) within 10 days of the date of this judgment. The parents must notify the court of any change in the information submitted within 10 days of the change, by filing an updated form. The Notice of Rights and Responsibilities—Health-Care Costs and Reimbursement Procedures and Information Sheet on Changing a Child Support Order (form FL-192) is attached.

Form Adopted Judicial Council
FL-180

4. 2340
3. 2340
5 ca.gov

CASE NAME (Last name, first name of each party)

CASE NUMBER
9D592793

HON. MICHELLE WILLIAMS COURT. DEPT. 57

4. i. [X] The children of this marriage or domestic partnership are:

(1) [X] Name

Birthdate
6/26/05
3/16/07

(2) [X] Parentage is established for children of this relationship born prior to the marriage or domestic partnership

j. [X] Child custody and visitation (parenting time) are ordered as set forth in the attached

(1) ☐ Settlement agreement, stipulation for judgment, or other written agreement which contains the information required by Family Code section 3048(a)

(2) ☐ Child Custody and Visitation Order Attachment (form FL-341).

(3) ☐ Stipulation and Order for Custody and/or Visitation of Children (form FL-355).

(4) [X] Previously established in another case. Case number: 6412FA000097 Court: WALWORTH COUNTY
STATE OF WISCONSIN CIRCUIT COURT

k. [X] Child support is ordered as set forth in the attached

(1) ☐ Settlement agreement, stipulation for judgment, or other written agreement which contains the declarations required by Family Code section 4065(a).

(2) ☐ Child Support Information and Order Attachment (form FL-342).

(3) ☐ Stipulation to Establish or Modify Child Support and Order (form FL-350).

(4) [X] Previously established in another case. Case number 6412FA000097 Court: WALWORTH COUNTY
STATE OF WISCONSIN CIRCUIT COURT

l. [X] Spousal, domestic partner, or family support is ordered

(1) ☐ Reserved for future determination as relates to ☐ petitioner ☐ respondent

(2) [X] Jurisdiction terminated to order spousal or partner support to [X] petitioner [X] respondent

(3) ☐ As set forth in the attached Spousal, Partner, or Family Support Order Attachment (form FL-343).

(4) ☐ As set forth in the attached settlement agreement, stipulation for judgment, or other written agreement.

(5) [X] Other (specify): SEE CONTINUATION OF JUDGMENT.

m. [X] Property division is ordered as set forth in the attached

(1) ☐ Settlement agreement, stipulation for judgment, or other written agreement.

(2) ☐ Property Order Attachment to Judgment (form FL-345)

(3) [X] Other (specify): SEE CONTINUATION OF JUDGMENT.

n. ☐ Attorney fees and costs are ordered as set forth in the attached

(1) ☐ Settlement agreement, stipulation for judgment, or other written agreement.

(2) ☐ Attorney Fees and Costs Order (form FL-346)

(3) ☐ Other (specify):

o. [X] Other (specify): SEE CONTINUATION OF JUDGMENT.

Each attachment to this judgment is incorporated into this judgment, and the parties are ordered to comply with each attachment's provisions. Jurisdiction is reserved to make other orders necessary to carry out this judgment.

Date:

5. Number of pages attached: 11

JUDICIAL OFFICER
[X] SIGNATURE FOLLOWS LAST ATTACHMENT

NOTICE

Dissolution or legal separation may automatically cancel the rights of a spouse or domestic partner under the other spouse's or domestic partner's will, trust, retirement plan, power of attorney, pay-on-death bank account, transfer-on-death vehicle registration, survivorship rights to any property owned in joint tenancy, and any other similar property interest. It does not automatically cancel the rights of a spouse or domestic partner as beneficiary of the other spouse's or domestic partner's life insurance policy. You should review these matters, as well as any credit cards, other credit accounts, insurance policies, retirement plans, and credit reports, to determine whether they should be changed or whether you should take any other actions.

A debt or obligation may be assigned to one party as part of the dissolution of property and debts, but if that party does not pay the debt or obligation, the creditor may be able to collect from the other party.

An earnings assignment may be issued without additional proof if child, family, partner, or spousal support is ordered.

Any party required to pay support must pay interest on overdue amounts at the "legal rate," which is currently 10 percent.

FL-180 [Rev

2 of 2

Pg 38

Exhibit 4

Copy of Birth Certificate of Beneficiary

Form CRB3

3180618

C\

DUPLICATE

REPUBLIC OF BOTSWANA

BIRTHS AND DEATHS REGISTRATION ACT, 1968

CERTIFICATE OF BIRTH
(Regulation 9)

1. Certificate Number ████████████

2. Registration Number ████████

3. Date of Birth   13th June 1989

4. Place of Birth   Selibe Phikwe Government, Selebi Phikwe

                             Selebi-Phikwe District, Botswana

5. Name(s)   ████████████

6. Sex   Female

7. Father's Name(s) and Surname ██████ ██████ ██████

8. Mother's Name(s) and Surname ██████ ██████

9. Date of Registration   27th April 2005

I hereby certify the above to be a true and correct extract from the Births Register kept at Gaborone in the Republic of Botswana.

Dated this   **21st**   day of   **November, 2016**

Pg 40

Exhibit 5

Copy of Passport of Beneficiary

NO STAMP, NO VISA LABEL ON THIS PAGE

REPUBLIC OF BOTSWANA

NATIONAL PASSPORT	Type/ Type **P**	Code/ Code **BWA**
PASSEPORT NATIONAL		

Surname/ Nom ▮

Prénoma

Nationality/ Nationalité ▮

Date of birth/ Date de naissance ▮

Sex/ Sexe
F

Date of issue/ Date de délivrance
12 SEP/SEPT 11

Date of expiry/ Date d'expiration
11 SEP/SEPT 21

Passport No./ N° de passeport ▮

Personal No./ N° personnel
866228319

Place of birth/ Lieu de naissance
SELEBI-PHIKWE

Authority/ Autorité
MLHA - DIC

Holder's signature/ Signature du titulaire

P<▮

BN01285116BWA8906131F2109114866228319<<<<<18

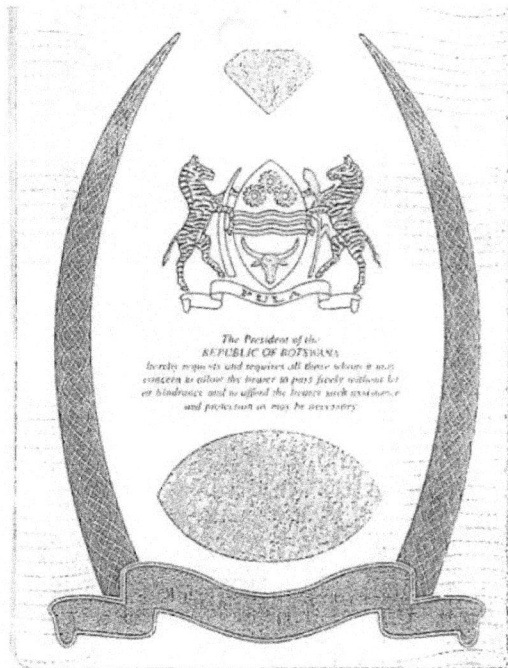

PASSPORT
PASSEPORT

**REPUBLIC OF
BOTSWANA**

This passport contains 48 pages
Ce passeport contient 48 pages

This passport is valid for
all countries of the world.

*Ce passeport est valide
pour tous les pays du monde.*

BN0128511

CERTIFIED TRUE COPY
OF THE ORIGINAL

Pg 43

Pg 44

Exhibit 6

Declaration Letter of the Petitioner and the Beneficiary

To whom it may concern:

I, ███ M. ███ I am 42 years old and currently reside in Long Beach, Ca.

I am writing this letter to tell the story of how I met ███ I joined a group on Facebook in May of 2017, the group is called "Love Sees No Colors" and is made up of people from all over the world. ███ was already in the group when I joined and we began to chat via Facebook Messenger. We had a few video calls after chatting and I was immediately taken by her beauty and intelligence. She was everything I had hoped for in a partner. Our relationship grew quickly and we talked almost daily. We began to make plans to meet in person. After looking into different types of visas and finding out what our options were, I decided to visit ███ in Botswana. I bought airline tickets to go see her in February of 2018. My flight left Los Angeles on February 9th and I arrived in Gaborone, Botswana on February 11th. ███ and her sister Kerry were waiting for me at the airport. It was one of the happiest moments of my life. After talking and planning for months we had finally met face to face. She was even more beautiful in person and I will never forget that day. The three of us went to ███ house where I met her daughters, Tasha and Sesame. They were a little shy at first but in no time we were getting along great. They are both very smart little girls and it gave me such joy to be around them. In the next few days ███ took me around Botswana and we I was able to meet more of her family and a few friends as well. They all made me feel so welcome, she has a wonderful family. Later in the week, on Valentines day, ███ her cousin, and myself drove out to a wild animal game reserve to give me a chance to see some real African wild animals. It was amazing, giraffe, zebra, kudu, impala and many more species that are native to Botswana. After the day at the reserve we took ███ cousin home and went back to the reserve for a romantic dinner in the bush. The park had set up tables and lights with music deep in the game reserve. It was the best Valentine's day dinner I have ever had. That is when I asked ███ to marry me and gave her an engagement ring. Thankfully she accepted and we are now doing everything we can tom make our dreams a reality. After Valentine's day we didn't have a lot of time left, I had to return to the United States to resume work. We spent the remainder of our time together relaxing and enjoying each others company. I flew back to Los Angeles on the 19th of February. It was hard to say goodbye to ███ and the girls. In the short amount of time we had we formed bonds and memories that will last a lifetime.

Since my return to the states we have been taking the steps to get married and begin our life together. We still talk everyday, and video chat almost as often. Our relationship continues to grow and I thank God every day for bringing us together. She is so incredibly smart and hard working, she takes care of her daughters and is one of the most responsible women I have ever met. There is so much I love about ███ She makes me laugh and smile almost every day, she is so incredibly beautiful, and she makes me want to work harder and be the best I can be. She speaks three languages and has a better understanding of English than I do, I am ever amazed by how smart ███ is and how hard she works. She is the perfect woman.

Date: September 28, 2018

_____
Matthew Michael Shimer

Pg 46

To whom it may concern:

I, ████████████ I am 29 years old and currently reside in Mmopane Block 1., Botswana.

I am writing this letter to tell the story of how I met ████ ████ In January 2017 I joined a dating group on Facebook called "Love sees no color", I joined it searching for a life partner. In that group that's where I met my handsome man ████ ████ Around May 2017, we started chatting on Facebook messenger. I can say that it was love at first sight the connection we had was beautiful and with every day that went by the with all the talking and video chatting we did the love started getting bigger and stronger.

At the beginning of February 2018, Matt told me that he was making plans to visit me so that we could meet in person. I couldn't believe it and since the excitement of knowing he was coming to see me was too much that I wanted to shared the new with everyone, I told my sister and called my parents to let them know that I was finally meeting the love of my life in person.

On February 11, 2018 Matt arrived in Botswana, My sister went went with me to pick him up at the airport. When I saw him I was speechless I couldn't believe that he was really there. In my eyes I saw a very smart and handsome man, I felt even more in love with him. It was for far one of the happiest days of my life.

The day he arrived we went to have dinner and spend all the days he was there together. The next day after his arrival he went to meet my children ████████. They were both very happy to finally meet him as well.

On February 14, 2018, ████ propose and I said yes! I was crying and nervous, but happy at the same time. Knowing that one day I will be Mrs. ████ and be by his side forever is one of my dreams.

Unfortunately my happiness didn't last long, on February 19, 2018. Matt went back to the US. and I had to stay home without him. Missing him and wishing I was with him.

████ ████ is a very loving and caring man, he loves my kids like they were his own. For the time we spent together he proved to me that he is going to be good father to my kids. I'm really grateful for the love he has to offer.

Date: September 28, 2018

Pg 47

Exhibit 7

Statement to Prove Intention to Marry
Within 90 Days of Arrival

To whom it may concern:

I, ████ M. ████ I am 42 years old and currently reside in Long Beach, Ca.

I am writing this letter to show my intentions to marry ████████ The moment that ████
████ arrives to the United States we will prepared everything needed to get married within 90
days of her arrival. That is my hope and prayer for the next chapter in our life together. It hasn't
been easy, all we can do sometimes is wait and pray that her visa gets approved, but I know
when we are finally together forever it will have been well worth the wait and preparation.

Date: September 28, 2018

_____

████████████

To whom it may concern:

I, ██████████████ am ready to get married to ████████ within 90 days of my arrival to the United States. I really pray that God helps us to accomplish all our future plans. I feel so blessed to have ████████ in my life, I love him so much and I can't wait to be with him forever.

Date: September 28, 2018

Exhibit 8

Proof of Communication Between Petitioner and
Beneficiary

Sprint

Call Details - (562) 987-0581 - Voice

On	At	To / From	Destination	Rate	Mins	Cost
Sep 18	07:46 am	(714) 918-6266	Incoming	WC/AU	05:00	-
	12:03 pm	(626) 234-8585	Incoming	WC/AU	03:00	-
	12:06 pm	(626) 234-8585	Incoming	WC/AU	01:00	-
	12:10 pm	(626) 234-8585	Incoming	WC/AU	01:00	-
	01:29 pm	(760) 978-7393	OCSD OCSD,CA	WC/AU	04:00	-
	02:20 pm	(580) 574-9982	Incoming	WC/AU	08:00	-
	03:20 pm	(714) 918-6266	Incoming	WC/AU	02:00	-
	03:27 pm	(714) 362-6581	HNTNGTNBCH,CA	WC/AU	02:00	-
	03:28 pm	(714) 404-2069	Incoming	CW/AU	01:00	-
	03:30 pm	(714) 404-2069	ANAHEIM,CA	WC/AU	23:00	-
Sep 19	08:22 am	(714) 918-6266	Incoming	WC/AU	02:00	-
	03:12 pm	(323) 489-6290	LOSANGELES,CA	AU	05:00	-
	03:28 pm	(562) 495-0554	LONG BEACH,CA	AU	04:00	-
	05:14 pm	(562) 337-4411	Incoming	WC/AU	01:00	-
	06:43 pm	(562) 277-4949	LONG BEACH,CA	NW,WC/AU	02:00	-
Sep 20	11:59 am	(213) 332-1821	Incoming	WC/AU	11:00	-
	02:05 pm	(951) 348-2064	Incoming	WC/AU	05:00	-
	06:13 pm	(562) 495-0554	LONG BEACH,CA	NW,AU	01:00	-
Sep 21	10:37 am	(714) 918-6266	SANTA ANA,CA	AU	02:00	-
	10:59 am	(714) 918-6266	Incoming	WC/AU	15:00	-
	11:55 am	(213) 332-1821	LOSANGELES,CA	WC/AU	02:00	-
	01:20 pm	(213) 332-1821	Incoming	WC/AU	01:00	-
Sep 22	06:29 am	(714) 362-6581	Incoming	NW/WC/AU	03:00	-
	01:04 pm	(714) 918-6266	Incoming	WC/AU	10:00	-
	01:15 pm	(213) 332-1821	LOSANGELES,CA	WC/AU	07:00	-
	02:05 pm	(714) 918-6266	Incoming	WC/AU	08:00	-
	02:37 pm	(916) 765-8140	Incoming	WC/AU	08:00	-
	03:37 pm	(714) 918-6266	Incoming	WC/AU	04:00	-
Sep 24	05:45 am	(562) 230-4797	Incoming	NW/WC/AU	25:00	-
Sep 25	04:27 am	(714) 362-6581	Incoming	NW/WC/AU	02:00	-
	04:36 am	(714) 362-6581	HNTNGTNBCH,CA	NW/WC/AU	01:00	-
	05:39 am	(213) 332-1821	Incoming	NW/WC/AU	07:00	-
	08:58 am	(714) 918-6266	Incoming	WC/AU	13:00	-
	09:35 am	(714) 918-6266	SANTA ANA,CA	AU	22:00	-
	11:15 am	(714) 918-6266	SANTA ANA,CA	AU	28:00	-
	03:04 pm	(562) 360-6266	Incoming	WC/AU	13:00	-
Sep 26	09:01 am	(714) 918-6266	SANTA ANA,CA	AU	20:00	-
	12:21 pm	(714) 918-6266	SANTA ANA,CA	AU	11:00	-
Sep 27	03:37 am	26777790770	Botswana-MOB	NW/LD	08:00	$2.96
	05:16 am	(213) 332-1821	Incoming	NW/WC/AU	01:00	-
	07:40 am	(626) 234-8585	Incoming	WC/AU	01:00	-
	07:53 am	(626) 234-8585	Incoming	WC/AU	02:00	-
	10:22 am	(626) 234-8585	Incoming	WC/AU	01:00	-
	10:48 am	(626) 234-8585	Incoming	WC/AU	02:00	-
	12:26 pm	(714) 918-6266	SANTA ANA,CA	AU	01:00	-
	01:35 pm	(626) 234-8585	ALHAMBRA,CA	WC/AU	02:00	-
	02:29 pm	(951) 348-2064	MURRIETA,CA	WC/AU	03:00	-
Sep 28	06:25 am	(626) 234-8585	ALHAMBRA,CA	NW/WC/AU	01:00	-
	08:42 am	(626) 234-8585	Incoming	WC/AU	01:00	-
	09:02 am	(626) 234-8585	Incoming	WC/AU	01:00	-
	03:13 pm	(626) 234-8585	Incoming	WC/AU	01:00	-

Rate Type

AU Anytime/Plan Usage

CW Call Waiting

LD Long Distance Charges

NW Night and Weekends

Pg 52

Sprint

Call Details - ▮▮▮▮▮ Voice ...continued

On	At	To / From	Destination	Rate	Mins	Cost
Sep 01	08:42 am	(951) 348-2064	MURRIETA,CA	WC/AU	02:00	-
	09:21 am	(951) 348-2064	Incoming	WC/AU	02:00	-
	11:11 am	(714) 918-6266	Incoming	WC/AU	04:00	-
	11:52 am	(714) 918-6266	SANTA ANA,CA	AU	02:00	-
	03:17 pm	(714) 918-6266	Incoming	WC/AU	02:00	-
	06:23 pm	(951) 348-2064	Incoming	NW/WC/AU	01:00	-
	06:24 pm	(866) 275-1411	Toll Free Call	NW/AU	02:00	-
	06:29 pm	(800) 877-4020	Toll Free Call	NW/AU	01:00	-
	06:37 pm	(951) 348-2064	MURRIETA,CA	NW/WC/AU	14:00	-
	06:52 pm	(714) 404-2069	ANAHEIM,CA	NW/WC/AU	02:00	-
	06:55 pm	(714) 404-2069	Incoming	NW/WC/AU	01:00	-
	07:09 pm	(714) 404-2069	ANAHEIM,CA	NW/WC/AU	31:00	-
Sep 02	07:55 am	(562) 360-6266	Incoming	NW/WC/AU	35:00	-
	09:19 am	(562) 360-6266	Incoming	NW/WC/AU	30:00	-
	11:24 am	(562) 833-5219	Incoming	NW/WC/AU	08:00	-
	06:46 pm	(424) 558-2060	Incoming	NW/WC/AU	04:00	-
Sep 03	06:31 am	(213) 922-8934	LOSANGELES,CA	NW/AU	08:00	-
	12:26 pm	(877) 959-1417	Incoming	NW/WC/AU	03:00	-
	07:29 pm	(562) 208-6923	ALAMITOS,CA	NW/WC/AU	05:00	-
	08:04 pm	(916) 765-8140	Incoming	NW/WC/AU	19:00	-
Sep 04	10:47 am	26775195561	Botswana-MOB	LD	01:00	$0.37
	10:51 am	(267) 368-5765	Botswana	LD	01:00	$0.29
	10:54 am	26775195561	Botswana-MOB	LD	03:00	$1.11
	01:23 pm	(562) 432-1676	LONG BEACH,CA	AU	02:00	-
	01:39 pm	(562) 432-1676	LONG BEACH,CA	AU	03:00	-
Sep 05	06:56 am	(714) 918-6266	Incoming	NW/WC/AU	02:00	-
	08:23 am	(714) 238-3434	ANAHEIM,CA	AU	07:00	-
	09:39 am	(800) 272-0180	Toll Free Call	AU	03:00	-
	10:11 am	(714) 918-6266	SANTA ANA,CA	AU	01:00	-
	10:23 am	(714) 404-2069	ANAHEIM,CA	WC/AU	04:00	-
	11:51 am	(800) 272-0180	Toll Free Call	AU	03:00	-
	11:53 am	(714) 918-6266	SANTA ANA,CA	AU	06:00	-
	12:05 pm	(714) 918-6266	SANTA ANA,CA	AU	03:00	-
	12:08 pm	(951) 348-2064	MURRIETA,CA	WC/AU	02:00	-
	12:12 pm	(951) 348-2064	Incoming	WC/AU	02:00	-
	02:18 pm	(580) 574-9982	Incoming	WC/AU	02:00	-
	02:20 pm	(714) 918-6266	SANTA ANA,CA	AU	02:00	-
	02:21 pm	(714) 918-6266	SANTA ANA,CA	AU	03:00	-
	02:42 pm	(714) 483-1797	Incoming	WC/AU	02:00	-
	02:45 pm	(951) 348-2064	Incoming	WC/AU	02:00	-
	02:58 pm	(714) 918-6266	SANTA ANA,CA	AU	07:00	-
	03:09 pm	(580) 574-9982	Incoming	WC/AU	04:00	-
	03:13 pm	(760) 712-5290	OCSD OCSD,CA	WC/AU	02:00	-
	03:14 pm	(714) 483-1797	Incoming	CW/AU	01:00	-
	03:15 pm	(714) 483-1797	SANTA ANA,CA	WC/AU	03:00	-
	03:30 pm	(760) 712-5290	OCSD OCSD,CA	WC/AU	15:00	-
	03:44 pm	(714) 918-6266	Incoming	CW/AU	25:00	-
	04:23 pm	(714) 981-7215	Incoming	WC/AU	02:00	-
Sep 06	06:32 am	(714) 483-1797	Incoming	WC/AU	03:00	-
	10:45 am	(714) 918-6266	SANTA ANA,CA	AU	03:00	-
	10:51 am	(714) 918-6266	SANTA ANA,CA	AU	03:00	-
	10:59 am	(714) 918-6266	SANTA ANA,CA	AU	01:00	-
	04:46 pm	(562) 296-6111	ALAMITOS,CA	AU	03:00	-

Sep
Ca

Rate Type

AU Anytime Plan Usage

CW Call Waiting

LD Long Distance Charges

NW Night and Weekends

Sprint

Call Details - ████████ - Voice ...continued

On	At	To / From	Destination	Rate	Mins	Cost
	01:42 am	26775195561	Botswana-MOB	NW/LD	03:00	$1.11
	01:46 am	26775195561	Botswana-MOB	NW/LD	09:00	$3.33
	09:35 am	(626) 234-8585	Incoming	WC/AU	01:00	-
	11:57 am	(714) 918-6266	Incoming	WC/AU	03:00	-
	12:03 pm	(714) 918-6266	SANTA ANA,CA	AU	10:00	-
	12:26 pm	(714) 404-2069	Incoming	WC/AU	12:00	-
	01:05 pm	(714) 918-6266	Incoming	WC/AU	03:00	-
	01:10 pm	(949) 701-2514	IRVINE,CA	WC/AU	06:00	-
	01:16 pm	(714) 918-6266	Incoming	WC/AU	23:00	-
	03:43 pm	(608) 266-1373	MADISON,WI	AU	01:00	-
Sep 30	08:38 am	(916) 765-8140	Incoming	NW/WC/AU	05:00	-
	09:35 am	(916) 765-8140	Incoming	NW/WC/AU	30:00	-
	01:09 pm	(562) 360-6266	WHITTIER,CA	NW/WC/AU	03:00	-
	02:15 pm	(562) 360-6266	Incoming	NW/WC/AU	13:00	-
Oct 02	09:04 am	(714) 918-6266	SANTA ANA,CA	AU	03:00	-
	09:23 am	(714) 918-6266	SANTA ANA,CA	AU	04:00	-
	11:54 am	(714) 918-6266	Incoming	WC/AU	05:00	-
	01:46 pm	(805) 368-3456	Incoming	WC/AU	04:00	-
	03:30 pm	(714) 918-6266	Incoming	WC/AU	01:00	-
	03:47 pm	(562) 405-7111	NORWALK,CA	WC/AU	02:00	-
	04:16 pm	(562) 230-4797	ALAMITOS,CA	WC/AU	01:00	-
	04:19 pm	(562) 230-4797	Incoming	WC/AU	06:00	-
Oct 03	09:34 am	(714) 404-2069	ANAHEIM,CA	WC/AU	33:00	-
	03:33 pm	(714) 918-6266	SANTA ANA,CA	AU	03:00	-
Oct 04	08:27 am	(714) 918-6266	Incoming	WC/AU	06:00	-
	05:23 pm	(951) 348-2064	MURRIETA,CA	WC/AU	07:00	-
	05:31 pm	(562) 360-6266	Incoming	WC/AU	04:00	-
	07:01 pm	(562) 360-6266	WHITTIER,CA	NW/WC/AU	01:00	-
Oct 05	09:42 am	(714) 918-6266	SANTA ANA,CA	AU	05:00	-
	10:19 am	(626) 234-8585	Incoming	WC/AU	03:00	-
	10:25 am	(714) 918-6266	SANTA ANA,CA	AU	10:00	-
	11:17 am	(626) 234-8585	Incoming	WC/AU	02:00	-
	05:33 pm	(262) 215-4300	LAKEGENEVA,WI	WC/AU	11:00	-
Oct 06	07:39 am	(714) 918-6266	SANTA ANA,CA	AU	08:00	-
	07:46 am	(714) 918-6266	Incoming	WC/AU	04:00	-
	07:52 am	(262) 325-5002	LAKEGENEVA,WI	WC/AU	22:00	-
	08:35 am	(562) 494-2296	ALAMITOS,CA	AU	04:00	-
	05:47 pm	(951) 870-0656	Incoming	WC/AU	14:00	-
Oct 07	02:25 pm	(562) 360-6266	WHITTIER,CA	NW/WC/AU	03:00	-
	04:37 pm	(562) 528-4194	LONG BEACH,CA	NW/WC/AU	02:00	-
	04:39 pm	(562) 360-6266	WHITTIER,CA	NW/WC/AU	02:00	-
	05:36 pm	(562) 528-4194	Incoming	NW/WC/AU	05:00	-
	06:07 pm	(562) 360-6266	Incoming	NW/WC/AU	24:00	-
	06:31 pm	(562) 360-6266	Incoming	NW/WC/AU	14:00	-
Oct 08	08:55 am	(562) 567-5318	WHITTIER,CA	NW/WC/AU	01:00	-
	03:43 pm	(562) 280-6372	Incoming	NW/WC/AU	02:00	-
Oct 09	06:43 pm	(562) 360-6266	Incoming	NW/WC/AU	23:00	-
Oct 10	01:45 pm	(562) 477-6996	Incoming	WC/AU	02:00	-
	04:13 pm	(562) 570-6622	LONG BEACH,CA	AU	01:00	-
	07:22 pm	(510) 393-2522	OKLD MN-PD,CA	NW/WC/AU	02:00	-
	07:26 pm	(562) 343-5388	ALAMITOS,CA	NW/AU	01:00	-
Oct 11	12:21 pm	(626) 234-8585	Incoming	WC/AU	01:00	-
Oct 12	03:09 pm	(262) 728-7000	DELAVAN,WI	WC/AU	02:00	-

Rate Type

AU Anytime Plan Usage

LD Long Distance
Charges

NW Night and Weekends

Co

Sprint

Call Details - ▮▮▮▮ Voice

On	At	To / From	Destination	Rate	Mins	Cost
Oct 19	03:09 pm	(714) 404-2069	Incoming	WC/AU	01:00	-
	03:11 pm	(714) 404-2069	ANAHEIM,CA	WC/AU	27:00	-
Oct 20	12:51 pm	(714) 918-6266	SANTA ANA,CA	A U	.03:00	-
	02:41 pm	(415) 686-2017	SAN RAFAEL,CA	WC/AU	01:00	-
	02:42 pm	(415) 686-2017	SAN RAFAEL,CA	WC/AU	13:00	-
	02:55 pm	(714) 483-1797	SANTA ANA,CA	WC/AU	03:00	-
Oct 23	10:52 am	(502) 416-1349	Incoming	WC/AU	01:00	-
Oct 24	01:19 pm	(206) 257-3880	Incoming	WC/AU	01:00	-
	01:20 pm	(206) 257-3880	SEATTLE,WA	AU	02:00	-
Oct 26	05:17 pm	(951) 348-2064	Incoming	WC/AU	19:00	-
Oct 27	01:51 pm	(714) 534-2700	Incoming	WC/AU	01:00	-
Oct 28	09:45 am	(562) 544-2969	Incoming	NW/WC/AU	02:00	-
	01:09 pm	(562) 607-7591	LONG BEACH,CA	NW/WC/AU	06:00	-
	01:48 pm	(562) 607-7591	LONG BEACH,CA	NW/WC/AU	03:00	-
	01:52 pm	(562) 607-7591	Incoming	NW/WC/AU	02:00	-
	02:35 pm	(562) 213-6382	LAKEWOOD,CA	NW/WC/AU	01:00	-
	02:44 pm	(562) 213-6382	Incoming	NW/WC/AU	02:00	-
	03:20 pm	(562) 213-6382	Incoming	NW/WC/AU	01:00	-
Oct 30	08:09 am	(714) 918-6266	SANTA ANA,CA	AU	01:00	-
	08:56 am	(714) 918-6266	Incoming	WC/AU	02:00	-
	11:53 am	(951) 348-2064	Incoming	WC/AU	02:00	-
Oct 31	02:48 pm	(714) 918-6266	SANTA ANA,CA	AU	02:00	-
	02:58 pm	(714) 918-6266	Incoming	WC/AU	04:00	-
Nov 01	04:52 pm	(562) 321-5016	Incoming	WC/AU	01:00	-
	06:16 pm	(562) 230-4797	ALAMITOS,CA	NW/WC/AU	03:00	-
Nov 02	12:01 pm	(562) 760-7357	Incoming	WC/AU	10:00	-
	02:51 pm	(562) 360-6266	Incoming	WC/AU	12:00	-
	03:17 pm	(562) 360-6266	Incoming	WC/AU	05:00	-
	03:29 pm	(562) 360-6266	WHITTIER,CA	WC/AU	03:00	-
Nov 03	07:59 am	(262) 215-4300	LA KEGENEVA,WI	WC/AU	16:00	-
	08:52 am	(800) 655-4555	Toll Free Call	AU	28:00	-
	09:54 am	(877) 959-1417	Incoming	WC/AU	01:00	-
Nov 05	01:11 pm	(562) 506-5463	LONG BEACH,CA	NW/WC/AU	26:00	-
Nov 07	11:47 am	(562) 606-0812	Incoming	WC/AU	01:00	-
Nov 08	07:56 pm	(951) 348-2064	Incoming	NW/WC/AU	21:00	-
Nov 10	11:20 am	(951) 348-2064	Incoming	WC/AU	00:00	-
	12:13 pm	26775195561	Botswana-MOB	LD	08:00	$2.96
	12:43 pm	(951) 348-2064	Incoming	WC/AU	01:00	-
	01:21 pm	(951) 348-2064	MURRIETA,CA	WC/AU	01:00	-
	02:55 pm	(562) 230-4797	ALAMITOS,CA	WC/AU	15:00	-
Nov 11	02:21 pm	(562) 606-0812	Incoming	NW/WC/AU	01:00	-
Nov 14	09:27 am	(714) 918-6266	SANTA ANA,CA	AU	02:00	-
	10:59 am	(415) 686-2017	SAN RAFAEL,CA	WC/AU	03:00	-
	12:05 pm	(310) 293-3219	CMTN GRDN,CA	WC/AU	02:00	-
	02:49 pm	(714) 918-6266	SANTA ANA,CA	AU	02:00	-
Nov 15	10:01 am	26775195561	Botswana-MOB	LD	02:00	$0.74
	07:04 pm	(626) 356-1000	PSDN MAIN,CA	NW/AU	01:00	-
	07:05 pm	(888) 512-5279	Toll Free Call	NW/AU	01:00	-
	07:06 pm	(888) 512-5279	Toll Free Call	NW/AU	04:00	-
Nov 16	07:25 am	(415) 686-2017	SAN RAFAEL,CA	WC/AU	01:00	-
	08:04 am	(714) 918-6266	Incoming	WC/AU	02:00	-
Nov			ALAMITOS,CA			

Rate Type

AU Anytime/Plan Usage

LD Long Distance Charges

NW Night and Weekends

Pg 55

![Sprint]

Call Details - ▓▓▓▓▓▓▓ - Voice

On	At	To / From	Destination	Rate	Mins	Cost
Nov 18	10:03 am	(424) 558-2060	TORRANCE,CA	NW/WC/AU	01:00	-
	11:03 am	(562) 436-1761	LONG BEACH, CA	NW/AU	04:00	-
	11:07 am	(951) 870-0656	CORONA,CA	NW/WC/AU	05:00	-
	03:24 pm	Unavailable	Incoming	NW/WC/AU	02:00	-
	06:07 pm	(424) 219-8622	Incoming	NW/WC/AU	13:00	-
Nov 20	08:24 am	(714) 918-6266	Incoming	WC/AU	03:00	-
	02:39 pm	(626) 234-8585	Incoming	WC/AU	06:00	-
	06:31 pm	(800) 887-8643	Toll Free Call	NW/AU	08:00	-
	07:30 pm	26775195551	Botswana-MOB	NW/LD	03:00	$1.11
Nov 21	06:33 am	(626) 234-8585	ALHAMBRA,CA	NW/WC/AU	01:00	-
	07:08 am	(310) 293-3219	Incoming	WC/AU	01:00	-
	01:09 pm	(310) 293-3219	Incoming	WC/AU	06:00	-
Nov 22	11:56 am	(714) 918-6266	SANTA ANA,CA	AU	03:00	-
Nov 23	02:58 pm	(424) 558-2060	Incoming	WC/AU	01:00	-
	03:09 pm	(562) 436-1761	LONG BEACH,CA	AU	02:00	-
Nov 24	05:42 am	(847) 651-5953	Incoming	NW/WC/AU	43:00	-
	01:23 pm	(206) 922-0865	Incoming	WC/AU	15:00	-
	02:44 pm	Unavailable	Incoming	WC/AU	02:00	-
	02:48 pm	(800) 833-9943	Toll Free Call	AU	12:00	-
Nov 25	10:00 am	(800) 833-9943	Toll Free Call	NW/AU	14:00	-
	10:14 am	(800) 742-5877	Toll Free Call	NW/AU	01:00	-
	10:16 am	(206) 922-0865	Incoming	NW/WC/AU	09:00	-
	12:59 pm	(562) 607-7591	Incoming	NW/WC/AU	05:00	-
	02:08 pm	(562) 607-7591	Incoming	NW/WC/AU	01:00	-
	02:58 pm	Unavailable	Incoming	NW/WC/AU	01:00	-
	03:32 pm	(562) 213-6382	Incoming	NW/WC/AU	02:00	-
	05:18 pm	(562) 541-3804	Incoming	NW/WC/AU	01:00	-
Nov 27	09:17 am	(714) 918-6266	SANTA ANA,CA	AU	05:00	-
	12:14 pm	(800) 275-8777	Toll Free Call	AU	04:00	-
Nov 28	09:43 am	(626) 234-8585	Incoming	WC/AU	04:00	-
	02:21 pm	(562) 326-8196	LONG BEACH,CA	WC/AU	06:00	-
	07:59 pm	(562) 230-4797	ALAMITOS,CA	NW/WC/AU	07:00	-
Nov 30	10:57 am	(415) 686-2017	Incoming	WC/AU	06:00	-
	12:18 pm	(951) 348-2064	Incoming	WC/AU	04:00	-
	03:29 pm	(562) 432-3530	LONG BEACH, CA	AU	03:00	-
Dec 01	03:49 am	(626) 356-1000	PSDN MAIN,CA	NW/AU	01:00	-
	03:51 am	(866) 400-5200	Toll Free Call	NW/AU	04:00	-
	09:54 am	(213) 321-3469	LOS ANGELES,CA	WC/AU	01:00	-
	09:55 am	(562) 360-6266	WHITTIER, CA	WC/AU	20:00	-
	10:18 am	(909) 243-7973	UPLAND,CA	AU	13:00	-
	01:16 pm	(562) 285-5050	LONG BEACH, CA	AU	08:00	-
	01:57 pm	(866) 400-5200	Toll Free Call	AU	07:00	-
	02:13 pm	(866) 400-5200	Incoming	WC/AU	01:00	-
	02:14 pm	(866) 400-5200	Toll Free Call	AU	08:00	-
	02:31 pm	(866) 400-5200	Incoming	WC/AU	02:00	-
	02:33 pm	(562) 360-6266	Incoming	WC/AU	14:00	-
Dec 02	08:32 am	(562) 360-6266	Incoming	NW/WC/AU	13:00	-
	10:59 am	(714) 362-6581	HNTNGTNBCH,CA	NW/WC/AU	01:00	-
	11:00 am	(714) 362-6581	Incoming	NW/WC/AU	01:00	-
	01:33 pm	(916) 765-8140	Incoming	NW/WC/AU	02:00	-
Dec 05	07:45 am	(626) 356-1000	PSDN MAIN,CA	AU	01:00	-
	07:46 am	(866) 400-5200	Toll Free Call	AU	03:00	-

Pg 56

Sprint

Call Details - ▌ - Voice ...continued

On	At	To / From	Destination	Rate	Mins	Cost
	07:57 am	(888) 512-5273	Toll Free Call	AU	01:00	
	04:17 pm	(425) 635-2370	Incoming	WC/AU	10:00	
Dec 06	10:42 am	(800) 275-8777	Toll Free Call	AU	02:00	
	10:45 am	(800) 275-8777	Toll Free Call	AU	05:00	
	10:49 am	(800) 275-8777	Toll Free Call	AU	59:00	
	05:37 pm	Unavailable	Incoming	WC/AU	02:00	
	06:30 pm	(800) 469-9269	Incoming	NW/WC/AU	02:00	
Dec 08	09:12 am	(385) 237-4427	Incoming	WC/AU	01:00	
	04:29 pm	(562) 296-6111	ALAMITOS,CA	AU	03:00	
Dec 11	08:00 am	(626) 234-8565	ALHAMBRA,CA	WC/AU	02:00	
	03:22 pm	(385) 237-4427	Incoming	WC/AU	01:00	
Dec 12	09:17 am	(626) 356-1000	PSDN MAIN,CA	AU	01:00	
	09:18 am	(626) 356-1000	PSDN MAIN,CA	AU	03:00	
Dec 13	09:37 am	(310) 293-3219	Incoming	WC/AU	07:00	
	09:30 am	(310) 293-3219	Incoming	WC/AU	01:00	
	10:12 am	(310) 293-3219	Incoming	WC/AU	05:00	
	11:46 am	20775195561	Incoming	WC/AU	14:00	
Dec 14	11:10 am	(562) 296-6111	Incoming	WC/AU	01:00	
	03:05 pm	(562) 350-6266	Incoming	WC/AU	43:00	
Dec 15	07:08 am	(562) 230-4797	ALAMITOS,CA	WC/AU	01:00	
	08:28 am	(562) 230-4797	Incoming	WC/AU	05:00	
	12:48 pm	(800) 444-4281	Toll Free Call	AU	21:00	
	04:48 pm	(562) 477-6046	LONG BEACH,CA	WC/AU	49:00	
	07:24 pm	(562) 616-2942	COMPTON,CA	NW/WC/AU	02:00	
	07:26 pm	(562) 833-5219	LONG BEACH,CA	NW/WC/AU	02:00	
	07:31 pm	(424) 558-2060	TORRANCE,CA	NW/WC/AU	02:00	
Dec 16	08:36 am	(877) 477-5807	Toll Free Call	NW/AU	02:00	
	09:31 am	(877) 477-5807	Toll Free Call	NW/AU	14:00	
	09:45 am	(800) 777-3999	Toll Free Call	NW/AU	05:00	
	09:50 am	(877) 477-5807	Toll Free Call	NW/AU	01:00	
	09:51 am	(877) 477-5807	Toll Free Call	NW/AU	16:00	
	02:54 pm	(562) 213-6382	LAKEWOOD,CA	NW/WC/AU	01:00	
	03:11 pm	(562) 213-6382	LAKEWOOD,CA	NW/WC/AU	01:00	

Rate Type
AU   Anytime/Plan Usage
NW   Night and Weekends

Sprint

Call Details - ██████████ - Voice

On	At	To / From	Destination	Rate	Mins	Cost
Feb 19	03:13 pm	(051) 870-0656	CORONA,CA	WC/AU	04:00	-
Feb 20	00:34 am	(714) 918-6266	SANTA ANA,CA	NW/AU	01:00	-
	07:09 am	(714) 918-6266	Incoming	WC/AU	05:00	-
	11:15 pm	(866) 400-5200	Toll Free Call	NW/VW/AU	11:00	-
	11:49 pm	(866) 400-5200	Incoming	NW/VW/AU	07:00	-
	11:58 pm	(866) 400-5200	Toll Free Call	NW/VW/AU	02:00	-
	11:58 pm	(866) 400-5200	Incoming	NW/VW/AU	10:00	-
Feb 21	12:14 am	(626) 356-1000	Incoming	NW/VW/AU	02:00	-
	12:16 am	(626) 356-1000	Incoming	NW/VW/AU	01:00	-
	12:58 pm	(866) 400-5200	Toll Free Call	AU	03:00	-
	03:27 pm	(800) 777-0133	Toll Free Call	AU	04:00	-
	03:30 pm	(800) 921-1117	Toll Free Call	AU	01:00	-
	03:32 pm	(800) 921-1117	Toll Free Call	AU	04:00	-
	03:36 pm	(800) 921-1117	Toll Free Call	AU	12:00	-
	06:37 pm	(562) 277-4949	Incoming	NW/WC/AU	15:00	-
Feb 23	08:00 am	(626) 234-8585	Incoming	WC/AU	01:00	-
	10:21 am	(626) 234-8585	Incoming	WC/AU	01:00	-
	03:28 pm	(916) 765-8140	Incoming	WC/AU	43:00	-
Feb 24	11:41 am	(562) 230-4797	ALAMITOS,CA	NW/WC/AU	04:00	-
Feb 26	12:21 pm	(714) 918-6266	SANTA ANA,CA	AU	03:00	-
	12:49 pm	26775195561	Botswana-MOB	LD	03:00	$1.11
	01:16 pm	(626) 234-8585	Incoming	WC/AU	05:00	-
	01:51 pm	(714) 918-6266	SANTA ANA,CA	AU	03:00	-
	01:54 pm	(626) 234-8585	Incoming	WC/AU	04:00	-
Feb 27	06:48 pm	(562) 213-6382	Incoming	NW/WC/AU	01:00	-
Mar 01	08:10 am	(714) 918-6266	SANTA ANA,CA	AU	03:00	-
	12:37 pm	(310) 293-3219	Incoming	WC/AU	11:00	-
Mar 02	10:52 am	(714) 918-6266	SANTA ANA,CA	AU	03:00	-
	11:58 am	(559) 362-7203	HANFORD,CA	WC/AU	27:00	-
	02:46 pm	(562) 495-0554	LONG BEACH,CA	AU	03:00	-
Mar 03	08:39 am	(661) 575-7868	PLDL PLDL,CA	NW/WC/AU	02:00	-
Mar 04	09:06 am	VoiceMail	ALAMITOS,CA	NW/AU	01:00	-
	09:07 am	(562) 360-6266	WHITTIER,CA	NW/WC/AU	13:00	-
	04:52 pm	(562) 326-8196	Incoming	NW/WC/AU	02:00	-
Mar 05	09:00 am	(978) 326-0970	Incoming	WC/AU	01:00	-
	02:10 pm	(714) 918-6266	SANTA ANA,CA	AU	12:00	-
	06:40 pm	(562) 760-7357	Incoming	NW/WC/AU	04:00	-
Mar 06	10:30 am	(877) 213-6452	Toll Free Call	AU	02:00	-
	11:34 am	(714) 918-6266	SANTA ANA,CA	AU	03:00	-
	07:38 pm	(562) 360-6266	Incoming	NW/WC/AU	15:00	-
Mar 08	08:12 am	(626) 234-8585	ALHAMBRA,CA	WC/AU	02:00	-
	08:14 am	(714) 918-6266	SANTA ANA,CA	AU	01:00	-
	08:18 am	(714) 918-6266	Incoming	WC/AU	28:00	-
	11:54 am	(626) 234-8585	ALHAMBRA,CA	WC/AU	17:00	-
Mar 09	09:48 am	(562) 495-0554	LONG BEACH,CA	AU	01:00	-
	09:48 am	(562) 495-0554	LONG BEACH,CA	AU	06:00	-
	09:56 am	(562) 495-0554	Incoming	WC/AU	01:00	-
	09:58 am	(562) 495-0554	Incoming	WC/AU	01:00	-
	10:48 am	(562) 495-0554	Incoming	WC/AU	03:00	-
	03:58 pm	(562) 230-4797	ALAMITOS,CA	WC/AU	10:00	-
Mar 10	07:18 am	Unavail abl	Incoming	NW/WC/AU	02:00	-
	11:26 am	26775195561	Botswana-MOB	NW/LD	21:00	$0.00

Mar

Call

Rate Type

AU Anytime Plan Usage

LD Long Distance
Charges

NW Night and Weekends

VW Wi-Fi Calling Calling
PLUS

WC Any Mobile Anytime

Sprint

Call Details - ▮▮▮▮▮ - Voice

On	At	To / From	Destination	Rate	Mins	Cost
Mar 18	07:21 am	26775195561	Botswana-MOB	NW/LD	20:00	$7.40
	01:38 pm	(877) 252-2701	Incoming	NW/WC/AU	02:00	·
	07:33 pm	(206) 922-0193	Incoming	NW/WC/AU	01:00	·
Mar 21	09:37 am	(805) 368-3456	Incoming	WC/AU	04:00	·
Mar 24	06:00 pm	Unavailable	Incoming	NW/WC/AU	02:00	·
Mar 28	10:44 am	(714) 918-6266	Incoming	WC/AU	04:00	·
	03:33 pm	(562) 477-8046	Incoming	WC/AU	14:00	·
Mar 29	10:29 am	(562) 310-0086	Incoming	WC/AU	02:00	·
	03:30 pm	(562) 477-8046	Incoming	WC/AU	07:00	·
	04:10 pm	(424) 328-1041	Incoming	WC/AU	04:00	·
Mar 30	08:29 am	(858) 204-2918	POWAY,CA	WC/AU	05:00	·
	09:17 am	(424) 328-1041	Incoming	WC/AU	03:00	·
	09:56 am	(424) 328-1041	LOMITA,CA	AU	01:00	·
	09:56 am	(424) 328-1041	LOMITA,CA	AU	01:00	·
	09:57 am	(424) 328-1041	Incoming	WC/AU	02:00	·
	10:18 am	(424) 328-1041	Incoming	WC/AU	01:00	·
	10:39 am	(424) 328-1041	LOMITA,CA	AU	01:00	·
	10:39 am	(424) 328-1041	LOMITA,CA	AU	01:00	·
	10:40 am	(424) 328-1041	Incoming	WC/AU	02:00	·
	10:44 am	(424) 328-1041	LOMITA,CA	AU	01:00	·
	12:13 pm	(562) 277-4949	LONG BEACH,CA	WC·AU	02:00	·
	12:17 pm	(562) 477-80 46	LONG BEACH,CA	WC/AU	01:00	·
	02:03 pm	(626) 234-8585	Incoming	WC/AU	04:00	·
	05:29 pm	(562) 477-8046	Incoming	WC/AU	02:00	·
Apr 02	06:11 am	(714) 918-6266	Incoming	NW/WC/AU	02:00	·
	08:21 am	(323) 217-4501	Incoming	WC/AU	02:00	·
	01:19 pm	(714) 918-6266	SANTA ANA,CA	AU	02:00	·
	01:25 pm	(714) 918-6266	Incoming	WC/AU	04:00	·
Apr 03	02:45 pm	(626) 234-8585	Incoming	WC/AU	36:00	·
	03:22 pm	(714) 404-2069	ANAHEIM,CA	WC/AU	01:00	·
	03:27 pm	(714) 313-8788	ANAHEIM,CA	WC/AU	08:00	·
	03:38 pm	(951) 348-2064	MURRIETA,CA	WC/AU	02:00	·
	03:51 pm	(714) 404-2069	Incoming	WC/AU	12:00	·
Apr 04	06:31 am	(626) 234-8585	Incoming	NW/WC/AU	08:00	·
	06:50 am	(951) 348-2064	Incoming	NW/WC/AU	07:00	·
	06:57 am	26775195561	Botswana-MOB	NW/LD	04:00	$1.48
Apr 05	04:17 pm	(562) 277-4949	Incoming	WC/AU	22:00	·
	04:45 pm	(951) 348-2064	MURRIETA,CA	WC/AU	26:00	·
Apr 06	08:14 am	(562) 495-0554	LONG BEACH,CA	AU	04:00	·
	10:48 am	(562) 453-7745	LONG BEACH,CA	WC/AU	02:00	·
Apr 07	09:56 am	(562) 453-7745	LONG BEACH,CA	NW/WC/AU	01:00	·
	07:15 pm	(424) 298-5678	Incoming	NW/WC/AU	06:00	·
	09:02 pm	(424) 298-5678	Incoming	NW/WC/AU	02:00	·
	09:26 pm	(424) 298-5678	Incoming	NW/WC/AU	01:00	·
	11:09 pm	(424) 298-5678	Incoming	NW/WC/AU	02:00	·
Apr 08	04:12 pm	(800) 342-5932	Toll Free Call	NW/AU	04:00	·
	04:22 pm	(800) 342-5932	Toll Free Call	NW/AU	04:00	·
Apr 09	07:11 am	(626) 234-8585	Incoming	WC/AU	02:00	·
	10:16 am	(714) 918-6266	SANTA ANA,CA	AU	04:00	·
	02:21 pm	(626) 234-8585	ALHAMBRA,CA	WC/AU	08:00	·
	03:17 pm	(562) 310-0086	LONG BEACH,CA	WC/AU	02:00	·
	03:26 pm	(562) 310-0086	Incoming	WC/AU	01:00	·

Rate Type

AU	Anytime Plan Usage
LD	Long Distance Charges
NW	Night and Weekends
WC	Any Mobile Anytime

Sprint

Call Details - ▓▓▓▓▓▓ - Voice ...continued

On	At	To / From	Destination	Rate	Mins	Cost
Apr 10	05:37 pm	(562) 495-0554	Incoming	WC/AU	03:00	-
	05:45 pm	(562) 495-0554	LONG BEACH,CA	AU	12:00	-
Apr 11	09:07 am	(626) 234-8585	ALHAMBRA,CA	WC/AU	06:00	-
	03:51 pm	(760) 978-7393	OCSD OCSD,CA	WC/AU	32:00	-
	06:13 pm	(424) 558-2060	TORRANCE,CA	NW/WC/AU	02:00	-
	06:14 pm	(562) 477-3319	Incoming	NW/CW/AU	02:00	-
	06:15 pm	(424) 558-2060	TORRANCE,CA	NW/WC/AU	01:00	-
Apr 12	10:51 am	(562) 277-4949	LONG BEACH,CA	WC/AU	13:00	-
	02:02 pm	26775195561	Botswana-MOB	LD	17:00	$6.29
	05:31 pm	(626) 234-8585	Incoming	WC/AU	20:00	-
Apr 13	07:54 am	26775195561	Botswana-MOB	LD	08:00	$2.96
	08:26 am	(562) 477-3319	LONG BEACH,CA	WC/AU	01:00	-
	08:27 am	(562) 477-3319	Incoming	WC/AU	02:00	-
	09:11 am	(562) 477-3319	Incoming	WC/AU	01:00	-
	09:31 am	(562) 477-3319	LONG BEACH,CA	WC/AU	01:00	-
Apr 14	10:03 am	(562) 591-2301	LONG BEACH,CA	NW/AU	06:00	-
	10:09 am	(562) 277-4949	LONG BEACH,CA	NW/WC/AU	04:00	-
	07:15 pm	(424) 298-5678	Incoming	NW/WC/AU	09:00	-
	09:49 pm	(424) 298-5678	Incoming	NW/WC/AU	01:00	-
Apr 16	05:44 am	(951) 348-2064	MURRIETA,CA	NW/WC/AU	05:00	-
	06:24 am	(626) 234-8585	Incoming	NW/WC/AU	06:00	-
	07:56 am	(714) 404-2069	ANAHEIM,CA	WC/AU	01:00	-
	08:15 am	(323) 217-4501	Incoming	WC/AU	04:00	-
	08:55 am	(714) 918-6266	Incoming	WC/AU	06:00	-
	09:10 am	26775195561	Botswana-MOB	LD	01:00	$0.37
	09:11 am	26775195561	Botswana-MOB	LD	01:00	$0.37
	09:55 am	(714) 404-2069	Incoming	WC/AU	20:00	-
	02:48 pm	26775195561	Botswana-MOB	LD	14:00	$5.18
Apr 17	10:09 am	(714) 918-6266	Incoming	WC/AU	06:00	-
	05:33 pm	(562) 810-1236	LONG BEACH,CA	WC/AU	02:00	-

Rate Type

AU Anytime/Plan Usage

CW Call Waiting

LD Long Distance
Charges

NW Night and Weekends

WC Any Mobile,Anytime

Sprint

Call Details - ██████████ - Voice

On	At	To / From	Destination	Rate	Mins	Cost
Apr 18	09:19 am	(951) 348-2064	Incoming	WC/AU	12.00	-
Apr 19	07:38 am	(626) 234-8585	Incoming	WC/AU	03.00	-
	02:52 pm	(610) 277-7575	NORRISTOWN,PA	AU	02.00	-
	03:55 pm	(562) 477-3319	Incoming	WC/AU	03.00	-
	05:25 pm	(626) 234-8585	Incoming	WC/AU	20.00	-
Apr 20	03:25 am	(562) 760-7357	LONG BEACH,CA	WC/AU	01.00	-
	08:59 am	(562) 453-7745	LONG BEACH,CA	WC/AU	01.00	-
	09:10 am	(562) 453-7745	Incoming	WC/AU	03.00	-
	10:47 am	(562) 505-9606	Incoming	WC/AU	17.00	-
	11:22 am	(562) 453-7745	Incoming	WC/AU	01.00	-
	01:11 pm	(714) 545-8010	SANTA ANA,CA	AU	01.00	-
	03:15 pm	(714) 545-8010	SANTA ANA,CA	AU	01.00	-
	03:52 pm	(714) 545-8010	Incoming	WC/AU	02.00	-
	04:33 pm	(424) 298-5676	Incoming	WC/AU	03.00	-
	05:23 pm	(562) 607-7591	Incoming	NW,WC/AU	14.00	-
Apr 21	11:25 am	26705195561	Incoming	NW,WC/AU	01.00	-
	11:28 am	26775195561	Botswana MOB	NW,LD	23.00	$8.51
Apr 22	01:33 pm	(310) 327-8571	CMTN GRDN,CA	NW/AU	02.00	-
	01:35 pm	(424) 244-4662	CMTN GRDN,CA	NW,WC/AU	01.00	-
	01:36 pm	(310) 733-0296	CULVER CITY,CA	NW,WC/AU	01.00	-
Apr 24	04:30 am	26775195561	Botswana MOB	NW,LD	17.00	$6.29
	11:18 am	(626) 234-8585	Incoming	WC/AU	03.00	-
Apr 25	10:16 am	(714) 918-6266	Incoming	WC/AU	02.00	-
	11:13 am	(714) 848-2112	Incoming	WC/AU	01.00	-
	12:04 pm	(424) 558-2060	TORRANCE,CA	WC/AU	06.00	-
	04:32 pm	26775195561	Incoming	WC/AU	01.00	-
	04:33 pm	26775195561	Botswana MOB	LD	02.00	$0.74
	04:36 pm	26775195561	Botswana MOB	LD	32.00	$11.84
	05:10 pm	Unavailable	Incoming	WC/AU	05.00	-
Apr 27	11:15 am	(562) 477-8046	Incoming	WC/AU	17.00	-
Apr 30	02:51 pm	(714) 628-4901	ORANGE,CA	AU	05.00	-
May 01	04:55 pm	(562) 619-1236	Incoming	WC/AU	02.00	-
	05:23 pm	(562) 619-1236	LONG BEACH,CA	WC/AU	02.00	-
	05:40 pm	(562) 619-1236	LONG BEACH,CA	WC/AU	01.00	-
	05:56 pm	(424) 296-5678	Incoming	WC/AU	03.00	-
May 02	08:55 am	(626) 234-5685	Incoming	WC/AU	03.00	-
	04:54 pm	(562) 277-4940	Incoming	WC/AU	36.00	-
May 03	09:34 am	(714) 916-6796	SANTA ANA,CA	AU	08.00	-
	09:41 am	(714) 404-2060	ANAHEIM,CA	WC/AU	07.00	-
	11:50 am	(714) 404-2060	Incoming	WC/AU	08.00	-
	09:20 pm	(951) 348-2064	MURRIETA,CA	WC/AU	01.00	-
	02:04 pm	(562) 277-4940	Incoming	WC/AU	09.00	-
	02:30 pm	(951) 348-2064	Incoming	NW,WC/AU	20.00	-
	06:08 pm	(580) 574-9942	LAWTON,OK	NW,WC/AU	13.00	-
May 04	07:05 am	(562) 277-4940	Incoming	WC/AU	06.00	-
	09:35 am	(562) 495-6954	LONG BEACH,CA	AU	04.00	-
	10:10 am	(424) 646-1960	ENGLEWOOD,CA	WC/AU	05.00	-
	09:30 am	(424) 646-1960	Incoming	WC/AU	02.00	-
May 06	09:21 am	(562) 230-4737	ALAMITOS,CA	NW,WC/AU	14.00	-
May 15	08:19 am	(424) 558-2060	TORRANCE,CA	NW,WC/AU	05.00	-
	01:47 pm	(562) 802-4748	Incoming	NW,WC/AU	15.00	-

Rate Type

AU Anytime Plan Usage

LD Long Distance
    Charges

NW Night and Weekends

Pg 61

Sprint

Call Details - ▮▮▮▮▮▮▮ - Voice ...continued

On	At	To / From	Destination	Rate	Mins	Cost
	01:26 pm	(323) 217-4501	Incoming	WC/AU	04.00	-
May 08	08.32 am	(323) 217-4501	Incoming	WC/AU	01.00	-
	10:40 am	(626) 234-8585	ALHAMBRA,CA	WC/AU	12.00	-
	11:45 am	(714) 918-6266	SANTA ANA,CA	AU	06.00	-
	04:58 pm	(562) 204-5223	Incoming	WC/AU	01.00	-
May 09	06:22 am	(714) 918-6266	SANTA ANA,CA	NW/AU	02.00	-
	03:07 pm	(562) 253-3600	LONG BEACH,CA	WC/AU	04.00	-
May 10	02:45 pm	(562) 204-5223	Incoming	WC/AU	02.00	-
	04:41 pm	(562) 277-4949	Incoming	WC/AU	20.00	-
May 11	04:15 am	26775195561	Botswana-MOB	NW/LD	01.00	50.37
	09:49 am	(562) 310-0086	Incoming	WC/AU	03.00	-
May 12	12:06 pm	(562) 204-5223	Incoming	NW/WC/AU	03.00	-
	03:06 pm	(562) 204-5223	WHITTIER,CA	NW/WC/AU	01.00	-
May 13	08:27 am	(424) 558-2060	Incoming	NW/WC/AU	02.00	-
May 14	02:22 pm	26777790770	Incoming	WC/AU	03.00	-
	02:51 pm	(714) 918-6266	Incoming	WC/AU	02.00	-
	04:33 pm	(714) 719-2379	GARDENGRV,CA	WC/AU	02.00	-
May 17	05:31 am	(951) 348-2064	Incoming	NW/WC/AU	17.00	-
	12:34 pm	(714) 918-6266	Incoming	WC/AU	03.00	-

Rate Type

AU Anytime/Plan Usage

LD Long Distance
    Charges

NW Night and Weekends

WC Any Mobile Anytime

Sprint

Call Details - [redacted] - Voice

Call time displays as Central Time (CT) or local time depending on how and where the call was made.

On	At	To / From	Destination	Rate	Mins	Cost
May 18	08:18 am	(562) 230-4797	ALAMITOS,CA	WC/AU	06:00	-
	08:52 am	(562) 436-7078	LONG BEACH,CA	AU	01:00	-
	08:53 am	(800) 325-6000	Toll Free Call	AU	04:00	-
	09:58 am	(714) 719-2379	Incoming	WC/AU	18:00	-
	10:15 am	(714) 313-8788	ANAHEIM,CA	WC/AU	01:00	-
	10:38 am	(714) 313-8788	Incoming	WC/AU	09:00	-
	02:44 pm	26777790770	Incoming	WC/AU	02:00	-
May 19	09:25 am	28775195561	Incoming	NW/WC/AU	09:00	-
May 20	09:22 am	(562) 230-4797	ALAMITOS,CA	NW/WC/AU	01:00	-
	09:23 am	(800) 253-4189	Toll Free Call	NW/AU	05:00	-
	09:59 am	(562) 230-4797	ALAMITOS,CA	NW/WC/AU	04:00	-
	01:35 pm	(562) 230-4797	Incoming	NW/WC/AU	01:00	-
	06:49 pm	(847) 651-5989	NORTHBROOK,IL	NW/WC/AU	16:00	-
May 21	08:26 am	(714) 918-6266	Incoming	WC/AU	03:00	-
	11:06 am	(714) 313-8788	Incoming	WC/AU	04:00	-
	11:58 am	(714) 362-6581	Incoming	WC/AU	03:00	-
	07:08 pm	(562) 204-5223	Incoming	NW/WC/AU	04:00	-
	07:14 pm	(562) 204-5223	WHITTIER,CA	NW/WC/AU	01:00	-
May 22	01:07 pm	(323) 587-3145	LOSANGELES,CA	AU	01:00	-
	01:10 pm	(323) 393-6630	LOSANGELES,CA	WC/AU	01:00	-
	01:22 pm	(714) 918-6266	SANTA ANA,CA	AU	04:00	-
May 23	06:46 am	(562) 477-3319	LONG BEACH,CA	NW/WC/AU	07:00	-
May 25	10:49 am	(562) 454-3645	Incoming	WC/AU	01:00	-
	11:16 am	(562) 454-3645	Incoming	WC/AU	01:00	-
May 26	12:24 pm	(951) 870-0656	Incoming	NW/WC/AU	01:00	-
May 27	07:34 am	(424) 376-4160	Incoming	NW/WC/AU	02:00	-
	02:39 pm	(310) 327-8571	CMTN GRDN,CA	NW/AU	03:00	-
	03:29 pm	26775195561	Incoming	NW/WC/AU	01:00	-
	08:14 pm	Unavailable	Incoming	NW/WC/AU	02:00	-
May 28	10:02 am	(562) 436-1761	LONG BEACH,CA	AU	02:00	-
	10:22 am	Unavailable	Incoming	WC/AU	02:00	-
	12:34 pm	(424) 376-4160	Incoming	WC/AU	01:00	-
	12:45 pm	(424) 376-4160	TORRANCE,CA	WC/AU	01:00	-
	12:46 pm	(424) 376-4160	TORRANCE,CA	WC/AU	01:00	-
	12:51 pm	(424) 376-4160	TORRANCE,CA	WC/AU	01:00	-
	12:55 pm	(424) 376-4160	Incoming	WC/AU	02:00	-
	01:38 pm	(562) 277-4949	Incoming	WC/AU	02:00	-
May 30	02:47 pm	(562) 495-0554	LONG BEACH,CA	AU	03:00	-
May 31	09:01 am	(844) 747-3860	Incoming	WC/AU	01:00	-
	09:54 am	(714) 918-6266	SANTA ANA,CA	AU	06:00	-
	06:00 pm	(562) 495-0554	Incoming	NW/WC/AU	02:00	-
Jun 02	09:25 am	(562) 477-3319	LONG BEACH,CA	NW/WC/AU	01:00	-
	09:26 am	(562) 477-3319	Incoming	NW/CW/AU	01:00	-
	09:37 am	(562) 477-33 9	LONG BEACH,CA	NW/WC/AU	01:00	-
Jun 04	05:22 pm	(562) 495-0554	Incoming	WC/AU	02:00	-
	05:40 pm	(562) 495-0554	Incoming	WC/AU	01:00	-
	05:52 pm	(973) 339-2600	Incoming	WC/AU	04:00	-
Jun 05	08:51 am	(651) 992-0404	Incoming	WC/AU	01:00	-
	10:40 am	(562) 495-0554	Incoming	WC/AU	11:00	-
Jun 06	09:30 am	(844) 211-6770	Toll Free Call	AU	08:00	-

Cal

Sprint

Call Details - ████████ - Voice ...continued

On	At	To / From	Destination	Rate	Mins	Cost
	10:45 am	(000) 000-0911	Emergency	FC	02:00	-
	11:27 am	(262) 325-5002	Incoming	WC/AU	05:00	-
	05:31 pm	(562) 495-0554	Incoming	WC/AU	08:00	-
Jun 08	11:19 am	(562) 495-0554	LONG BEACH,CA	AU	05:00	-
	11:25 am	(847) 651-5989	NORTHBROOK,IL	WC/AU	04:00	-
	11:38 am	(262) 215-4300	LAKEGENEVA,WI	WC/AU	05:00	-
	01:04 pm	(949) 701-2514	IRVINE,CA	WC/AU	10:00	-
	08:48 pm	Unavailable	Incoming	NW/WC/AU	01:00	-
Jun 11	07:14 am	(714) 918-6266	SANTA ANA,CA	AU	07:00	-
	07:53 am	(949) 701-2514	Incoming	WC/AU	01:00	-
	08:42 am	(714) 918-6266	Incoming	WC/AU	03:00	-
	05:09 pm	(562) 495-0554	Incoming	WC/AU	07:00	-
Jun 12	01:42 pm	26775195561	Incoming	WC/AU	06:00	-
	03:06 pm	26775195561	Botswana-MOB	LD	03:00	$1.11
Jun 13	07:40 am	(714) 918-6266	SANTA ANA,CA	AU	11:00	-
	08:07 am	(714) 497-5960	Incoming	WC/AU	06:00	-
	01:34 pm	(562) 760-7357	Incoming	WC/AU	02:00	-
	01:40 pm	(562) 760-7357	Incoming	WC/AU	09:00	-
	01:51 pm	(323) 821-2220	LOSANGELES,CA	WC/AU	03:00	-
	01:55 pm	(714) 918-6266	SANTA ANA,CA	AU	06:00	-
	02:13 pm	(714) 918-6266	SANTA ANA,CA	AU	02:00	-
	02:30 pm	(714) 918-6266	Incoming	WC/AU	09:00	-
Jun 14	08:49 am	(714) 918-6266	SANTA ANA,CA	AU	08:00	-
	01:01 pm	(262) 325-5002	LAKEGENEVA,WI	WC/AU	05:00	-
	05:53 pm	(562) 495-0554	Incoming	WC/AU	09:00	-
Jun 15	08:42 am	(714) 403-8688	Incoming	WC/AU	04:00	-
	08:59 am	(760) 978-7393	OCSD OCSD,CA	WC/AU	04:00	-
	10:00 am	26775195561	Botswana-MOB	LD	10:00	$3.70
	01:34 pm	(714) 403-8688	Incoming	WC/AU	04:00	-
	04:00 pm	(424) 558-2060	TORRANCE,CA	WC/AU	03:00	-
	04:13 pm	(562) 337-1787	LONG BEACH,CA	WC/AU	02:00	-
Jun 17	09:02 am	(424) 558-2060	TORRANCE,CA	NW/WC/AU	01:00	-

Rate Type

AU Anytime/Plan Usage

FC Free Call

LD Long Distance Charges

NW Night and Weekends

WC Any Mobile,Anytime

Pg 64

Exhibit 9

Proof that Petitioner and Beneficiary Have Met
Each Other in Person

Pg 66

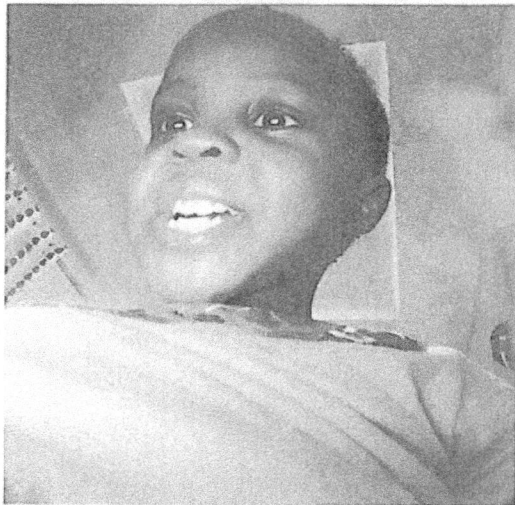

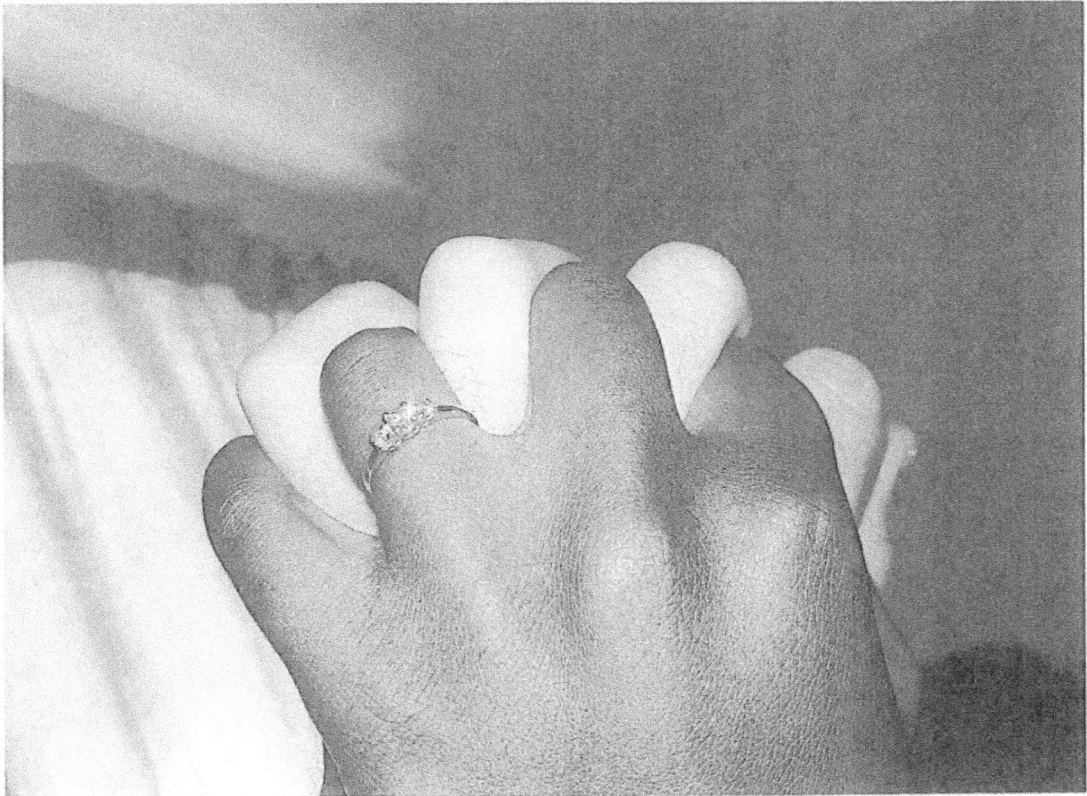

Pg 71

Pg 72

Pg 73

Pg 75

Pg 76

Pg 77

Pg 78

Pg 79

Pg 81

Exhibit 10

Copy of Airline Tickets and Itinerary of
Petitioner

SOUTH AFRICAN AIRWAY

BOARDING TIME
1045

FLIGHT 1767 JOHANNESBURG
GABORONE

GATE   SEAT 5B
                SEQ004

FLIGHT COUPON REQUIRED
BOARDING PASS

SOUTH AFRICAN AIRWAY

NAME ▬▬▬▬▬▬
11FEB
FQTV
FLIGHT 1767 SEQ004

GATE   SEAT
            5B
BOARDING TIME 1045

DEP JNB 1130
ARR GBE 1220

Y/S 5B

ECONOMY CLASS
SHIMEP/MATTHEW MIC
SA 1767 11FEB
FROM JOHANNESBURG
TO   GABORONE

DEPARTURE TIME 11:30

SEAT:
5B

CLASS:
Y/S

ECONOMY CLASS
SHIMER/MATTHEW MIC
SA 1767 18FEB
FROM GABORONE/GBE
TO   JOHANNESBURG/J

DEPARTURE TIME: 12:55

ETKT 10837207617622S
SEQ NO: 25
1/12KG

SEAT:
57C

CLASS:
Y/G

ECONOMY CLASS
SHIMER/MATTHEW MIC
SA 209 18FEB
FROM JOHANNESBURG/J
TO   WASHINGTON/IAD

DEPARTURE TIME: 18:50

ETKT 10837207617622S
SEQ NO: 87
1/12KG

BOARDING PASS:

FLIGHT NO	BOARDING TIME	GATE	SEAT	CLASS	SEAT
VX1089	07:23	B63	23D	Y/S	23D

NAME ▬▬▬▬▬▬
FROM WASHINGTON/IAD
TO   LOS ANGELES/LAX

CLASS: Y/S
DATE: 19FEB

VX 1089 19FEB
FROM WASHINGTON/IAD
TO   LOS ANGELES/LA

DEPARTURE TIME: 08:03

Pg 84

Exhibit 11

Support Letters of Friends and Relative of
Petitioner and Beneficiary

June 15, 2018

To whom it may concern,

My name is Skyler Dorsett and I am a US citizen. I have been friends with
███████ ██████ for 29 years. We were childhood friends who moved out from
Wisconsin to California together in our early 20's and have always maintained a close
friendship.

Matt met ████████████ on Facebook just over a year ago on a group page
they were both a part of. They realized how much they had in common and became
fast friends, talking to each other every day. It was clear to my wife and me from early
on that they had a special connection. I have never, in all my years knowing Matt, seen
him this excited about anyone before. It's been wonderful to see Matt happy and
connected. Matt speaks of ████████ children with fondness and proudly shares
pictures of them as if they were his own.

Matt and ███████ made plans for her to come out and visit him in California in
August of last year and I was with him the night he found out that she would be unable
to make the trip. It was obvious how devastated they both were to be unable to meet in
person, but they continued talking daily until he was able to visit her and meet her family
in Botswana in February. This was when he asked her to marry him. Their fondness
for eachother is obvious and they interact every day, showing so much care, concern
and respect for each other.

To whom it may concern,

We are writing to let you know that we are aware of our son Matthew's relationship with Tshepo Tawana. We support this relationship as we realize they have come to know and care for each other in a special way. His feelings for her are evident and they are committed to building a life together as they seek the best way to look forward to meeting Tshepo and being supportive of them as a couple.

Sincerely,

Bill and Jan Shimer
N 3675 Oak Hill St
Delavan, Wisconsin
53115

6/13/18

Matt ███████ is one of my dearest friends. His loyalty, compassion, and integrity are unsurpassable. I am thrilled that Matt and ███████ found each other and I wholeheartedly support their relationship.   My wife and I look forward to the day we get to meet her in person.

Sincerely,

Skyer Dorsett

4447 Tulane Ave.

Long Beach, Ca 90808

Exhibit 12

Copy of Employment Letter of Petitioner

COAST SURVEYING, INC.
15031 PARKWAY LOOP, SUITE B, TUSTIN, CA 92780-6527   (714) 918-6266   FAX (714) 918-6277
www.coastsurvey.com

July 13, 2018

To whom it may concern,

This letter is to verify that ███████ ████ is currently employed by Coast Surveying, Inc. He has been employed by Coast Surveying, Inc. since July 29, 2015.

Sincerely,

Ken Kasbohm, PLS 7371
Survey Manager

Exhibit 13

Copy of Paycheck Stubs of Petitioner

ast Surveying, Inc.
031 Parkway Loop, Suite B
istin, CA 92780
1: (714) 918-6266,

Earnings Statement

		Employee Number	22

		Check Date:	May 18, 2018
		Period Beginning:	April 29, 2018
		Period Ending:	May 12, 2018
Department	2	Voucher Number	2122
Classifica	400	Net Pay	2,045.68

arnings	Rate	Hours	Amount	YTD Hrs	YTD Amt
:G	50.91	64.00	3258.24	608.00	30953.28
r	76.36	16.00	1221.84	152.00	11607.48
VAC	0.00		269.60		2561.20
otal Gross Pay		80.00	4749.68	760.00	45121.96

Taxes	Status	Taxable	Amount	YTD Am
Medicare		4749.68	68.87	654.2
OASDI		4749.68	294.48	2797.5
CA SDI - Employee		4749.68	47.50	451.2
Federal Income Tax	S/1	4649.68	823.83	7884.1
California SITW	S/1	4649.68	342.35	3201.0
Total Tax Withholding			1577.03	14988.1

Deductions	Amount	YTD Am
401k Regular	100.00	800.0
Union Vacation Out	269.60	2561.2
Wisconsin Child Support	757.37	7573.7
Total Deductions	1126.97	10934.9

irect Deposits	Account		Amount
xxx1627	xxxxx8256		2045.68
otal Direct Deposits			2045.68

enefits	Hours	Amount	YTD Hrs	YTD Amt

Accruals	Hour
CASCK	24.0

REMOVE DOCUMENT ALONG THIS PERFORATION

oast Surveying, Inc.
5031 Parkway Loop, Suite B
ustin, CA 92780
H: (714) 918-6266,

This is not a check

Direct Deposit Voucher

10819 2-400   22 2123 5

236 Atlantic Avenue, #3
Long Beach, CA 90802

Direct Deposit Advice
Check Date   Voucher Number
May 18, 2018   2123

oast Surveying, Inc.
5031 Parkway Loop, Suite B
ustin, CA 92780
H: (714) 918-6266,

						Check Date:	May 04, 20.
						Period Beginning:	April 15, 20.
						Period Ending:	April 28, 20:

Matthew ▉▉▉   Employee Number   22 | Department | 2 | Voucher Number | 20I |
| Classifica | 400 | Net Pay | 2,045.(|

Earnings	Rate	Hours	Amount	YTD Hrs	YTD Amt
EG	50.91	64.00	3258.24	544.00	27695.04
T	76.36	16.00	1221.84	136.00	10385.64
NVAC	0.00		269.60		2291.60
Total Gross Pay		80.00	4749.68	680.00	40372.28

Taxes	Status	Taxable	Amount	YTD A
Medicare		4749.68	68.87	585.
OASDI		4749.68	294.48	2503.
CA SDI - Employee		4749.68	47.49	403.
Federal Income Tax	S/1	4649.68	823.83	7060.
California SITW	S/1	4649.68	342.35	2858.
Total Tax Withholding			1577.02	13411.

Deductions	Amount	YTD A
401k Regular	100.00	700.
Union Vacation Out	269.60	2291.
Wisconsin Child Support	757.37	6816.
Total Deductions	1126.97	9807.

Direct Deposits	Account	Amount
xxxx1627	xxxxx8256	2045.69
Total Direct Deposits		2045.69

Benefits	Hours	Amount	YTD Hrs	YTD Amt

Accruals		Hou
CASCK		24.0

REMOVE DOCUMENT ALONG THIS PERFORATION

Coast Surveying, Inc.
15031 Parkway Loop, Suite B
Tustin, CA 92780
PH: (714) 918-6266,

Direct Deposit Advice
Check Date   Voucher Numbe
May 04, 2018   208

This is not a check
Direct Deposit Voucher

▉▉▉▉▉

236 Atlantic Avenue, #3
Long Beach, CA 90802

Coast Surveying, Inc.
15031 Parkway Loop, Suite B
Tustin, CA 92780
PH: (714) 918-6266,

		Check Date:	June 29, 21
		Period Beginning:	June 10, 20
		Period Ending:	June 23, 20
Department	2	Voucher Number	22
Classifica	400	Net Pay	2,045.

Employee Number 22

Earnings	Rate	Hours	Amount	YTD Hrs	YTD Amt
REG	50.91	64.00	3258.24	800.00	40728.00
OT	76.36	16.00	1221.84	200.00	15273.00
UNVAC	0.00		269.60		3370.00
Total Gross Pay		80.00	4749.68	1000.00	59371.00

Taxes	Status	Taxable	Amount	YTD A
Medicare		4749.68	68.87	860
OASDI		4749.68	294.48	3681
CA SDI - Employee		4749.68	47.50	593
Federal Income Tax	S/1	4649.68	823.83	10355
California SITW	S/1	4649.68	342.35	4228
Total Tax Withholding			1577.03	19719

Deductions	Amount	YTD A
401k Regular	100.00	1100
Union Vacation Out	269.60	3370
Wisconsin Child Support	757.37	9845
Total Deductions	1126.97	14315

Direct Deposits	Account	Amount
xxxxx1627	xxxxx8256	2045.68
Total Direct Deposits		2045.68

Benefits	Hours	Amount	YTD Hrs	YTD Amt

Accruals		Hou
CASCK		24

Coast Surveying, Inc.
15031 Parkway Loop, Suite B
Tustin, CA 92780
PH: (714) 918-6266,

Direct Deposit Advice
Check Date Voucher Numbe
June 29, 2018 222

This is not a check
Direct Deposit Voucher

236 Atlantic Avenue, #3
Long Beach, CA 90802

Exhibit 14

Copy of 2016-2017 Income Tax Returns
and W2 Form of Petitioner

REPORT OF TAXABLE UNEMPLOYMENT COMPENSATION PAYMENTS FROM THE STATE OF CALIFORNIA

2017

Form 1099G Rev. 34

T A B L E A

Employment Development Department Unemployment Insurance Integrity and Accounting Division - MIC 16A P.O. Box 2408 Rancho Cordova, CA 95741-2408	Recipient's Name ▓▓▓ M ▓▓▓		Social Security Number ▓▓▓▓
Payer's Federal ID No. 94-2650401 1. Unemployment Compensation (UC) $1,774	2. State or Local Income Tax Refunds, Credits, or Offsets	3. Box 2 Amount is for Tax Year	4. Federal Income Tax Withheld $178
	Type of UC Payments UI $ 1,774	2017 Benefits Repaid (a) $0.00 Prior Year(s) Benefits Repaid (b) $0.00	

This is important tax information and is being furnished to the Internal Revenue Service (IRS). If you are required to file a return, a negligence penalty or other sanction may be imposed on you if this income is taxable and the IRS determines that it has not been reported.

FORM 1099G CERTAIN GOVERNMENT PAYMENTS

REPORT OF TAXABLE UNEMPLOYMENT COMPENSATION-PAID FAMILY LEAVE PAYMENTS FROM THE STATE OF CALIFORNIA

OMB NO. 1545-0120

2017

Form 1099G Rev. 34

T A B L E B

Employment Development Department Unemployment Insurance Integrity and Accounting Division - MIC 16A P.O. Box 2408 Rancho Cordova, CA 95741-2408	Recipient's Name ▓▓▓ M ▓▓▓		Social Security Number ▓▓▓▓
Payer's Federal ID No. 94-2650401 1. Unemployment Compensation-Paid Family Leave (UC-PFL) $0.00	2. State or Local Income Tax Refunds, Credits, or Offsets	3. Box 2 Amount is for Tax Year	4. Federal Income Tax Withheld $0.00
	PFL Payments $0.00	2017 Benefits Repaid (a) $0.00	

Pg 96

From the California Franchise Tax Board

STATE OF CALIFORNIA FRANCHISE TAX BOARD PO BOX 942840 SACRAMENTO CA 94240-0040	RECIPIENT'S Identification number ▓▓▓▓	2. State or local income tax refunds, credits, or offsets $ 2,772.00	OMB No. ▓▓▓▓ **2017** FORM 1099-G
Payer's FEIN 68-0204061	3. Tax year 2016		

RECIPIENT'S name ▓▓▓▓ M ▓▓▓▓

IMPORTANT TAX DOCUMENT
THIS FORM IS FOR YOUR RECORDS - DO NOT ATTACH WITH YOUR TAX RETURN

INSTRUCTIONS TO RECIPIENT

Box 2. Shows refunds, credits, or offsets of state or local income tax you received. It may be taxable to you if you deducted the state or local income tax paid on Schedule A (Form 1040). Even if you did not receive the amount shown, for example, because it was credited to your state or local estimated tax, it is still taxable if it was deducted. If you received interest on this amount, you should receive Form 1099-INT for the interest. However, the payer may include interest of less than $600 in the blank box on Form 1099-G. Regardless of whether the interest is reported to you, report it as interest income on your tax return. See your tax return for instructions.

NOTE: THIS IS IMPORTANT TAX INFORMATION AND IS BEING FURNISHED TO THE INTERNAL REVENUE SERVICE. IF YOU ARE REQUIRED TO FILE A RETURN, A NEGLIGENCE PENALTY OR OTHER SANCTION MAY BE IMPOSED ON YOU IF THIS INCOME IS TAXABLE AND THE IRS DETERMINES THAT IT HAS NOT BEEN REPORTED.

For information on how to report the refund amount shown, please refer to the instructions in your state and federal tax booklets when filing your tax return. For information about this notice, call us at the appropriate telephone number listed below.

Telephone: 800.852.5711 from within the United States
916.8
TTY/

Pg 97

Top Left W-2:

a Employee's social security number: 389-80-6856	1 Wages, tips, other comp. 102678.77	2 Federal income tax withheld 19826.71
Employer ID number 33-0017362	3 Social security wages 102678.77	4 Social security tax withheld 6366.08
	5 Medicare wages and tips 102678.77	6 Medicare tax withheld 1488.84

c Employer's name, address, and ZIP code

Coast Surveying, Inc.
15031 Parkway Loop Suite B
Tustin, CA 92780

Control Number
10819 22

e Employee's first name and initial — Last name

Matthew ▮
236 Atlantic Avenue, #3
Long Beach, CA 90802

f Employee's address, and ZIP code

7 Social security tips	8 Allocated tips	9
10 Dependent care benefits	11 Nonqualified plans	12a Code
13 Statutory employee 14 Other CASDI 924.11		12b Code
Retirement plan		12c Code
3rd party sick pay		12d Code

CA ▮	102678.77	6967.73

15 State Emplr.'s state I.D. # | 16 State wages, tips, etc. | 17 State income tax
18 Local wages, tips, etc. | 19 Local income tax | 20 Locality name

Form W-2 Wage and Tax Statement   Dept. of the Treasury - IRS
This information is being furnished to the Internal Revenue Service

Top Right W-2:

a Employee's social security number 389-80-6856	1 Wages, tips, other comp. 102678.77	19826.71
b Employer ID number 33-0017362	3 Social security wages 102678.77	4 Social security tax withheld 6366.08
	5 Medicare wages and tips 102678.77	6 Medicare tax withheld 1488.84

c Employer's name, address, and ZIP code

Coast Surveying, Inc.
15031 Parkway Loop Suite B
Tustin, CA 92780

d Control Number
10819 22

e Employee's first name and initial — Last name

▮ ▮
236 Atlantic Avenue, #3
Long Beach, CA 90802

f Employee's address, and ZIP code

7 Social security tips	8 Allocated tips	9
10 Dependent care benefits	11 Nonqualified plans	12a Code
13 Statutory employee 14 Other CASDI 924.11		12b Code
Retirement plan		12c Code
3rd party sick pay		12d Code

CA ▮	102678.77	6967.73

15 State Emplr.'s state I.D. # | 16 State wages, tips, etc. | 17 State income tax
18 Local wages, tips, etc. | 19 Local income tax | 20 Locality name

Form W-2 Wage and Tax Statement   Dept. of the Treasury - IRS
This information is being furnished to the IRS. If you are required to file a tax return, a negligence penalty/other sanction may be imposed on you if this income is taxable and you fail to report it

Bottom Left W-2:

Copy 2 To Be Filed With Employee's State, City, or Local Income Tax Return   **2017** OMB No. 1545-0008

a Employee's social security number ▮	1 Wages, tips, other comp. 102678.77	2 Federal income tax withheld 19826.71
b Employer ID number ▮	3 Social security wages 102678.77	4 Social security tax withheld 6366.08
	5 Medicare wages and tips 102678.77	6 Medicare tax withheld 1488.84

c Employer's name, address, and ZIP code

Coast Surveying, Inc.
15031 Parkway Loop Suite B
Tustin, CA 92780

d Control Number
10819 22

e Employee's first name and initial — Last name

▮ ▮
236 Atlantic Avenue, #3
Long Beach, CA 90802

f Employee's address, and ZIP code

7 Social security tips	8 Allocated tips	9
10 Dependent care benefits	11 Nonqualified plans	12a Code
13 Statutory employee 14 Other CASDI 924.11		12b Code
Retirement plan		12c Code
3rd party sick pay		12d Code

CA ▮		

Bottom Right W-2:

Extra Employee Copy   **2017** OMB No. 1545-0008

a Employee's social security number ▮	1 Wages, tips, other comp. 102678.77	2 Federal income tax withheld 19826.71
b Employer ID number ▮	3 Social security wages 102678.77	4 Social security tax withheld 6366.08
	Medicare wages and tips 102678.77	6 Medicare tax withheld 1488.8?

c Employer's name, address, and ZIP code

Coast Surveying, Inc.
15031 Parkway Loop Suite B
Tustin, CA 92780

d Control Number
10819 22

e Employee's first name and initial — Last name

▮ ▮
236 Atlantic Avenue, #3
Long Beach, CA 90802

f Employee's address, and ZIP code

7 Social security tips	8 Allocated tips	9
10 Dependent care benefits	11 Nonqualified plans	12a Code
13 Statutory employee 14 Other CASDI 924.11		12b Code
Retirement plan		12c Code
3rd party sick pay		12d Code

67.73

Form 1040 Department of the Treasury—Internal Revenue Service (99)

U.S. Individual Income Tax Return **2017**

For the year Jan. 1–Dec. 31, 2017, or other tax year beginning _____, 2017, ending _____, 20____   See separate instructions.

Your first name and initial: ▋ M   Last name: ▋   Your social security number: ▋

If a joint return, spouse's first name and initial: _____   Last name: _____   Spouse's social security number: _____

Home address (number and street). If you have a P.O. box, see instructions. ▋   Apt. no. 3

City, town or post office, state, and ZIP code. If you have a foreign address, also complete spaces below (see instructions).
LONG BEACH CA 90802

Foreign country name: _____   Foreign province/state/county: _____   Foreign postal code: _____

▲ Make sure the SSN(s) above

Presidential Election Campaign
Check here if you, or your spouse if filing jointly, want $3 to go to this fund. Checking a box below will not change your tax or refund. ☐ You ☐ Spouse

Filing Status
Check only one box.

1 ☐ Single
2 ☐ Married filing jointly (even if only one had income)
3 ☐ Married filing separately. Enter spouse's SSN above and full name here. ▶
4 ☒ Head of household (with qualifying person). (See instructions.) If the qualifying person is a child but not your dependent, enter this child's name here. ▶
5 ☐ Qualifying widow(er) (see instructions)

Exemptions

6a ☒ Yourself. If someone can claim you as a dependent, do not check box 6a . . . . .
b ☐ Spouse . . . .

c Dependents:

(1) First name Last name	(2) Dependent's social security number	(3) Dependent's relationship to you	(4) ✓ if child under age 17 qualifying for child tax credit (see instructions)
CHARLOTTE I ▋	▋	Daughter	☒
			☐
			☐
			☐

If more than four dependents, see instructions and check here ▶ ☐

Boxes checked on 6a and 6b: **1**
No. of children on 6c who:
• lived with you: **1**
• did not live with you due to divorce or separation (see instructions): ____
Dependents on 6c not entered above: ____
Add numbers on lines above ▶ **2**

d Total number of exemptions claimed . . . .

Income

Attach Form(s) W-2 here. Also attach Forms W-2G and 1099-R if tax was withheld.

If you did not get a W-2, see instructions.

7	Wages, salaries, tips, etc. Attach Form(s) W-2	**7** 102,679.
8a	Taxable interest. Attach Schedule B if required	**8a**
b	Tax-exempt interest. Do not include on line 8a [8b]	
9a	Ordinary dividends. Attach Schedule B if required	**9a**
b	Qualified dividends [9b]	
10	Taxable refunds, credits, or offsets of state and local income taxes	**10** 1,233.
11	Alimony received	**11**
12	Business income or (loss). Attach Schedule C or C-EZ	**12**
13	Capital gain or (loss). Attach Schedule D if required. If not required, check here ▶ ☐	**13**
14	Other gains or (losses). Attach Form 4797	**14**
15a	IRA distributions [15a] b Taxable amount	**15b**
16a	Pensions and annuities [16a] b Taxable amount	**16b**
17	Rental real estate, royalties, partnerships, S corporations, trusts, etc. Attach Schedule E	**17**
18	Farm income or (loss). Attach Schedule F	**18**
19	Unemployment compensation	**19** 1,774.
20a	Social security benefits [20a] b Taxable amount	**20b**
21	Other income. List type and amount _____	**21**
22	Combine the amounts in the far right column for lines 7 through 21. This is your total income ▶	**22** 105,686.

Adjusted Gross Income

23	Educator expenses	**23**
24	Certain business expenses of reservists, performing artists, and fee-basis government officials. Attach Form 2106 or 2106-EZ	**24**
25	Health savings account deduction. Attach Form 8889	**25**
26	Moving expenses. Attach Form 3903	**26**
27	Deductible part of self-employment tax. Attach Schedule SE	**27**
28	Self-employed SEP, SIMPLE, and qualified plans	**28**
29	Self-employed health insurance deduction	**29**
30	Penalty on early withdrawal of savings	**30**
31a	Alimony paid b Recipient's SSN ▶ _____	**31a**
32	IRA deduction	**32**
33	Student loan interest deduction	**33**
34	Reserved for future use	**34**

Form 1040 Department of the Treasury—Internal Revenue Service (99)

U.S. Individual Income Tax Return

2016 OMB No. 1545-0074 | IRS Use Only—Do not write or staple in this space.

For the year Jan. 1–Dec. 31, 2016, or other tax year beginning _____ , 2016, ending _____ , 20 _____

See separate instructions.

Your first name and initial	Last name	Your social security number
▮ M	▮	389-80-6856

If a joint return, spouse's first name and initial | Last name | Spouse's social security number

Home address (number and street). If you have a P.O. box, see instructions. | Apt. no.

236 ATLANTIC AVE. | 3

▲ Make sure the SSN(s) above and on line 6c are correct.

City, town or post office, state, and ZIP code. If you have a foreign address, also complete spaces below (see instructions).

LONG BEACH CA 90802

Foreign country name | Foreign province/state/county | Foreign postal code

Presidential Election Campaign
Check here if you, or your spouse if filing jointly, want $3 to go to this fund. Checking a box below will not change your tax or refund. ☐ You ☐ Spouse

Filing Status

Check only one box.

1 ☐ Single
2 ☐ Married filing jointly (even if only one had income)
3 ☐ Married filing separately. Enter spouse's SSN above and full name here. ►
4 ☒ Head of household (with qualifying person). (See instructions.) If the qualifying person is a child but not your dependent, enter this child's name here. ►
5 ☐ Qualifying widow(er) with dependent child

Exemptions

6a ☒ Yourself. If someone can claim you as a dependent, do not check box 6a .
b ☐ Spouse

c Dependents:

(1) First name Last name	(2) Dependent's social security number	(3) Dependent's relationship to you	(4) ✓ if child under age 17 qualifying for child tax credit (see instructions)
▮ ▮	▮	Daughter	☒
			☐
			☐
			☐

If more than four dependents, see instructions and check here ► ☐

d Total number of exemptions claimed .

Boxes checked on 6a and 6b — 1
No. of children on 6c who:
• lived with you — 1
• did not live with you due to divorce or separation (see instructions) — ___
Dependents on 6c not entered above — ___
Add numbers on lines above ► 2

Income

Attach Form(s) W-2 here. Also attach Forms W-2G and 1099-R if tax was withheld.

If you did not get a W-2, see instructions.

7	Wages, salaries, tips, etc. Attach Form(s) W-2 .	7	84,564.
8a	Taxable interest. Attach Schedule B if required .	8a	
b	Tax-exempt interest. Do not include on line 8a .	8b	
9a	Ordinary dividends. Attach Schedule B if required .	9a	
b	Qualified dividends .	9b	
10	Taxable refunds, credits, or offsets of state and local income taxes .	10	2,056.
11	Alimony received .	11	
12	Business income or (loss). Attach Schedule C or C-EZ .	12	
13	Capital gain or (loss). Attach Schedule D if required. If not required, check here ► ☐	13	
14	Other gains or (losses). Attach Form 4797 .	14	
15a	IRA distributions . 15a	b Taxable amount .	15b	
16a	Pensions and annuities 16a	b Taxable amount .	16b	
17	Rental real estate, royalties, partnerships, S corporations, trusts, etc. Attach Schedule E	17	
18	Farm income or (loss). Attach Schedule F .	18	
19	Unemployment compensation .	19	1,006.
20a	Social security benefits 20a	b Taxable amount .	20b	
21	Other income. List type and amount _____	21	
22	Combine the amounts in the far right column for lines 7 through 21. This is your total income ►	22	87,626.

Adjusted Gross Income

23	Educator expenses .	23	
24	Certain business expenses of reservists, performing artists, and fee-basis government officials. Attach Form 2106 or 2106-EZ	24	
25	Health savings account deduction. Attach Form 8889 .	25	
26	Moving expenses. Attach Form 3903 .	26	
27	Deductible part of self-employment tax. Attach Schedule SE	27	
28	Self-employed SEP, SIMPLE, and qualified plans .	28	
29	Self-employed health insurance deduction .	29	
30	Penalty on early withdrawal of savings .	30	
31a	Alimony paid b Recipient's SSN ►	31a	
32	IRA deduction .	32	
33	Student loan interest deduction .	33	
34	Tuition and fees. Attach Form 8917 .	34	

Exhibit 15

Copy of Conviction Records of
Petitioner.

NO. 9LM04667   PAGE NO. 1
THE PEOPLE OF THE STATE OF CALIFORNIA   VS.   CURRENT DATE 06/08/18
DEFENDANT 01: ███████████████████
LAW ENFORCEMENT AGENCY EFFECTING ARREST: LONG BEACH POLICE DEPT.

BAIL: APPEARANCE AMOUNT   DATE   RECEIPT OR SURETY COMPANY   REGISTER
      DATE   OF BAIL   POSTED   BOND NO.   NUMBER

CASE FILED ON 06/05/99.
 COMPLAINT FILED, DECLARED OR SWORN TO CHARGING DEFENDANT WITH HAVING
COMMITTED, ON OR ABOUT 02/12/99 IN THE COUNTY OF LOS ANGELES, THE FOLLOWING
OFFENSE(S) OF:
  COUNT 01: 487(A) PC MISD
NEXT SCHEDULED EVENT:
  06/22/99   830 AM ARRAIGNMENT   DIST LONG BEACH COURTHOUSE DIV 002

ON 06/22/99 AT 830 AM IN LONG BEACH COURTHOUSE DIV 002

CASE CALLED FOR ARRAIGNMENT
PARTIES: CMR JEFFERY P. CASTNER (JUDGE) ELOUISE MARTINEZ (CLERK)
              NONE   (REP) NONE (DDA)
DEFENDANT IS NOT PRESENT IN COURT, AND NOT REPRESENTED BY COUNSEL
 BENCH WARRANT ORDERED/ISSUED
NEXT SCHEDULED EVENT:
WARRANT ISSUED & CLDR CANCEL

06/22/99 BENCH WARRANT IN THE AMOUNT OF $26,000.00 BY ORDER OF JUDGE CMR
    JEFFERY P. CASTNER ISSUED. (06/25/99).

ON 06/28/99 AT 800 AM IN LONG BEACH COURTHOUSE DIV CRM

CASE CALLED FOR MISCELLANEOUS
PARTIES: NONE (JUDGE) ROSEMARIE RIVERA (CLERK)
              NONE   (REP) NONE (CP)
DEFENDANT IS PRESENT IN COURT, AND NOT REPRESENTED BY COUNSEL
 BENCH WARRANT RECALLED

  WALK-IN P.M. COURT.
NEXT SCHEDULED EVENT:
  06/28/99   830 AM BENCH WARRANT HEARING   DIST LONG BEACH COURTHOUSE DIV
   002

ON 06/28/99 AT 830 AM IN LONG BEACH COURTHOUSE DIV 002

CASE CALLED FOR BENCH WARRANT HEARING
PARTIES: CMR JEFFERY P. CASTNER (JUDGE) SHIRLEY MYERS (CLERK)
              DOROTHY DA ROZA (REP)   DAVID A. GORDON (CP)
PUBLIC DEFENDER APPOINTED. A ECONOMU - P.D.
DEFENDANT IS PRESENT IN COURT, AND REPRESENTED BY A ECONOMU DEPUTY PUBLIC
 DEFENDER
DEFENDANT STATES HIS/HER TRUE NAME AS CHARGED.
DEFENDANT ADVISED OF THE FOLLOWING RIGHTS ORALLY:
 DEFENDANT ARRAIGNED, AND ADVISED OF THE FOLLOWING RIGHTS: PLEAS
  AVAILABLE TO DEFENDANT; EXPLANATION OF NOLO CONTENDERE PLEA; TO

THE AID OF AN ATTORNEY AT ALL STAGES OF THE PROCEEDINGS; TO A
REASONABLE LENGTH OF TIME TO CONSULT AN ATTORNEY: THAT THE
COURT WOULD APPOINT AN ATTORNEY FREE OF CHARGE IF DEFENDANT DOES
NOT HAVE THE FINANCIAL MEANS TO RETAIN OWN; THAT UPON CONCLUSION
OF THE CASE, THE COURT MAY ORDER A HEARING TO DETERMINE THE
DEFENDANT'S THEN ABILITY TO PAY FOR ALL OR ANY PART OF THE COST
OF APPOINTED COUNSEL, AND THAT DEFENDANT MAY BE ORDERED TO PAY
ALL OR THAT PART OF SAID COSTS WITHIN DEFENDANT'S ABILITY TO
PAY, RIGHT TO REPRESENT HIMSELF IN PRO PER AND ADVISED OF
DISADVANTAGES OF SELF REPRESENTATION; NO SPECIAL TREATMENT BY
COURT; PROSECUTOR EXPERIENCED ATTORNEY; CANNOT LATER CLAIM ERROR
FOR INADEQUACY OF REPRESENTATION; THE DEFENDANT HAS BEEN ADVISED
THAT THERE MAY BE DEFENSES THAT HE/SHE IS UNAWARE OF; TO PUBLIC
TRIAL BY JURY OR COURT IN LONG BEACH; TO DISMISSAL IF NOT TRIED
WITHIN 30 DAYS IF IN CUSTODY; WITHIN 45 DAYS IF NOT; TO THE AID
OF THE COURT TO SUBPOENA AND PRODUCE WITNESSES ON OWN BEHALF; TO
REASONABLE BAIL PENDING TRIAL; TO CONFRONT AND EXAMINE ADVERSE
WITNESSES; TO EXERCISE PRIVILEGE AGAINST SELF INCRIMINATION AND

REMAIN SILENT; INFORMED THAT BY ENTERING A PLEA OF GUILTY, THESE
RIGHTS WOULD BE WAIVED; ADVISED RIGHT TO BE SENTENCED IN NOT
LESS THAN 6 HOURS OR MORE THAN 5 DAYS UNLESS REFERRED TO THE
PROBATION OFFICE; ADVISED MAXIMUM SENTENCE, UNLESS COURT
INDICATED OTHERWISE, WOULD BE 1 YEAR COUNTY JAIL, $1,000 FINE OR
BOTH; ADVISED MEANING OF PROBATION AND POSSIBLE OF LATER
SENTENCE IF COURT DETERMINES VIOLATION; ADVISED IF ON PROBATION
TO ANOTHER COURT THAT PLEA/CONVICTION MAY RESULT IN REVOCATION;
THE RIGHT TO HAVE A JUDGE REVIEW THE EVIDENCE TO DETERMINE IF
THERE IS PROBABLE CAUSE TO KEEP THE DEFENDANT IN CUSTODY UNTIL
TRIAL, THAT CONVICTION OF THE OFFENSE MAY HAVE THE CONSEQUENCES
OF DEPORTATION, EXCLUSION FROM ADMISSION TO THE UNITED STATES,
OR DENIAL OF NATURALIZATION
A COPY OF THE COMPLAINT AND THE ARREST REPORT GIVEN TO DEFENDANTS COUNSEL.
DEFENDANT PLEADS NOT GUILTY TO COUNT 01, 487(A) PC.
NEXT SCHEDULED EVENT:
 UPON MOTION OF DEFENDANT
07/09/99   830 AM PRETRIAL HEARING   DIST LONG BEACH COURTHOUSE DIV P/T

06/28/99 BENCH WARRANT IN THE AMOUNT OF $26,000.00   RECALLED. (06/28/99).

CUSTODY STATUS: RELEASED ON OWN RECOGNIZANCE

ON 07/09/99 AT 830 AM IN LONG BEACH COURTHOUSE DIV P/T

CASE CALLED FOR PRETRIAL HEARING
PARTIES: JOHN H. ING (JUDGE) VALERIE TAYLER (CLERK)
                CINDY ROSALES   (REP) JAMES YOUNG (CP)
DEFENDANT IS PRESENT IN COURT, AND REPRESENTED BY ANN T. NGUYEN DEPUTY PUBLIC
 DEFENDER
NEXT SCHEDULED EVENT:
 08/02/99   830 AM JURY TRIAL   DIST LONG BEACH COURTHOUSE DIV J/T

CUSTODY STATUS: RELEASED ON OWN RECOGNIZANCE

ON 08/02/99 AT 830 AM IN LONG BEACH COURTHOUSE DIV J/T

CASE CALLED FOR JURY TRIAL
PARTIES: GARY J. FERRARI (JUDGE) BETTY JENNINGS (CLERK)
                THERESE CLAUSSEN (REP)   PAUL S. ROBBINS (CP)

DEFENDANT IS PRESENT IN COURT, AND REPRESENTED BY THOMAS M. TYLER DEPUTY PUBLIC
   DEFENDER

A PLEA OF NOLO CONTENDERE SHALL BE CONSIDERED THE SAME AS A PLEA OF GUILTY.
   FOR THE PURPOSES OF THE CRIMINAL PROCEEDING, IT IS AN ADMISSION OF GUILT BUT
   CANNOT BE USED AGAINST YOU AS AN ADMISSION OF FAULT IN A CIVIL PROCEEDINGS
   ARISING OUT OF THE INCIDENT THAT CAUSED CRIMINAL PROCEEDINGS TO BE BROUGHT;

DEFENDANT ADVISED OF AND PERSONALLY AND EXPLICITLY WAIVES THE FOLLOWING RIGHTS:
TRIAL BY COURT AND TRIAL BY JURY
   CONFRONTATION AND CROSS-EXAMINATION OF WITNESSES;
   SUBPOENA OF WITNESSES INTO COURT TO TESTIFY IN YOUR DEFENSE;
   AGAINST SELF-INCRIMINATION;
DEFENDANT ADVISED OF THE FOLLOWING:
  THE NATURE OF THE CHARGES AGAINST HIM, THE ELEMENTS OF THE OFFENSE IN THE
   COMPLAINT, AND POSSIBLE DEFENSES TO SUCH CHARGES;
  THE POSSIBLE CONSEQUENCES OF A PLEA OF GUILTY OR NOLO CONTENDERE, INCLUDING
   THE MAXIMUM PENALTY AND ADMINISTRATIVE SANCTIONS AND THE POSSIBLE LEGAL

   EFFECTS AND MAXIMUM PENALTIES INCIDENT TO SUBSEQUENT CONVICTIONS FOR THE
   SAME OR SIMILAR OFFENSES;
  THE EFFECTS OF PROBATION;
  IF YOU ARE NOT A CITIZEN, YOU ARE HEREBY ADVISED THAT A CONVICTION OF THE
   OFFENSE FOR WHICH YOU HAVE BEEN CHARGED MAY HAVE THE CONSEQUENCES OF
   DEPORTATION, EXCLUSION FROM ADMISSION TO THE UNITED STATES, OR DENIAL OF
   NATURALIZATION PURSUANT TO THE LAWS OF THE UNITED STATES.
COUNSEL FOR THE DEFENDANT JOINS IN THE WAIVERS AND CONCURS IN THE PLEA.
COURT FINDS THAT EACH SUCH WAIVER IS KNOWINGLY, UNDERSTANDINGLY, AND EXPLICITLY
   MADE;
THE DEFENDANT PERSONALLY WITHDRAWS PLEA OF NOT GUILTY TO COUNT 01 AND PLEADS
   NOLO CONTENDERE WITH THE APPROVAL OF THE COURT TO A VIOLATION OF SECTION
   487(A) PC IN COUNT 01. THE COURT FINDS THE DEFENDANT GUILTY.
COUNT (01) : DISPOSITION: CONVICTED
COURT ACCEPTS PLEA
NEXT SCHEDULED EVENT:
   SENTENCING
   DEFENDANT WAIVES ARRAIGNMENT FOR JUDGMENT AND STATES THERE IS NO LEGAL CAUSE
   WHY SENTENCE SHOULD NOT BE PRONOUNCED. THE COURT ORDERED THE FOLLOWING
   JUDGMENT:
AS TO COUNT   (01):

IMPOSITION OF SENTENCE SUSPENDED
DEFENDANT PLACED ON SUMMARY PROBATION
   FOR A PERIOD OF 003 YEARS UNDER THE FOLLOWING TERMS AND CONDITIONS:
   PLUS $35.00 INSTALLMENT & ACCOUNTS RECEIVABLE FEE (PURSUANT TO 1205(D)PC)
   PERFORM 45 DAYS OF CAL TRANS
   DEFENDANT SHALL PAY RESTITUTION IN THE AMOUNT OF $100.00 TO RESTITUTION FINE.
      THROUGH THE COURT
      TOTAL DUE: $135.00
   IN ADDITION:
   -COURT ORDERS DEFENDANT TO REPORT FOR FINANCIAL EVALUATION
      PURSUANT TO 987.8 P.C.
   OBEY ALL LAWS AND FURTHER ORDERS OF THE COURT.
   DEFT. TO PAY REST. IN THE AMOUNT OF $1084.00 DIRECTLY TO THE
   VICTIM AND SUBMIT PROOF TO COURT ON 120299.
COUNT (01): DISPOSITION: CONVICTED

DMV ABSTRACT NOT REQUIRED
NEXT SCHEDULED EVENT:
  12/02/99   830 AM RESTITUTION HEARING   DIST LONG BEACH COURTHOUSE DIV FER

ON 08/04/99 AT 800 AM :

  REC'D ASSESSMENT AGREEMENT AND WAIVER FORM. FJ
  RESTITUTION HEARING

ON 12/02/99 AT 830 AM IN LONG BEACH COURTHOUSE DIV FER

CASE CALLED FOR RESTITUTION HEARING
PARTIES: GARY J. FERRARI (JUDGE) BETTY JENNINGS (CLERK)
              THERESE CLAUSSEN   (REP) CALVIN GEORGE (CP)

DEFENDANT IS PRESENT IN COURT, AND REPRESENTED BY THOMAS M. TYLER DEPUTY PUBLIC
  DEFENDER
  PROGRESS REPORT ON RESTITUTION AND STAY FOR C/S 030200 FER.
NEXT SCHEDULED EVENT:
  03/02/00   830 AM PROGRESS REPORT   DIST LONG BEACH COURTHOUSE DIV FER

ON 03/02/00 AT 830 AM IN LONG BEACH COURTHOUSE DIV FER

CASE CALLED FOR PROGRESS REPORT
PARTIES: GARY J. FERRARI (JUDGE) BETTY JENNINGS (CLERK)
              THERESE CLAUSSEN   (REP) CALVIN GEORGE (CP)
DEFENDANT IS PRESENT IN COURT, AND REPRESENTED BY THOMAS M. TYLER DEPUTY PUBLIC
   DEFENDER
  STAY ON C/S; REST. FINE; AND RESTITUTION TO 062800 D/FER.
  COURT ORDERS AND FINDINGS:
  -THE COURT ORDERS THE DEFENDANT TO APPEAR ON THE NEXT COURT DATE.
NEXT SCHEDULED EVENT:
  06/28/00   830 AM PROOF OF RESTITUTION   DIST LONG BEACH COURTHOUSE DIV FER

CUSTODY STATUS: DEFENDANT REMAINS ON OWN RECOGNIZANCE

ON 06/28/00 AT 830 AM IN LONG BEACH COURTHOUSE DIV FER

CASE CALLED FOR PROOF OF RESTITUTION
PARTIES: TOMSON T ONG (JUDGE) IMELDA EVANCULLA (CLERK)
              LYNNE FRANKO   (REP) SANDRA L. STOLPE (CP)
DEFENDANT IS PRESENT IN COURT, AND NOT REPRESENTED BY COUNSEL
  DEFENDANT APPEARS IN PRO PER
  BALANCE OF RESTITUTION, AND PROOF OF COMMUNITY SERVICE.
  DEFENDANT HAS PAID $650 OF $1084.
  COURT ORDERS AND FINDINGS:
  -THE COURT ORDERS THE DEFENDANT TO APPEAR ON THE NEXT COURT DATE.
NEXT SCHEDULED EVENT:
  10/30/00   830 AM PROGRESS REPORT   DIST LONG BEACH COURTHOUSE DIV FER

ON 10/30/00 AT 830 AM IN LONG BEACH COURTHOUSE DIV FER

CASE CALLED FOR PROGRESS REPORT
PARTIES: GARY J. FERRARI (JUDGE) IMELDA EVANCULLA (CLERK)
                THERESE CLAUSSEN   (REP) DAVID A. GORDON (CP)
DEFENDANT IS PRESENT IN COURT, AND NOT REPRESENTED BY COUNSEL
  DEFENDANT APPEARS IN PRO PER
  COURT ORDERS AND FINDINGS:
  -THE COURT ORDERS THE DEFENDANT TO APPEAR ON THE NEXT COURT DATE.
NEXT SCHEDULED EVENT:
  02/28/01 830 AM PROGRESS REPORT   DIST LONG BEACH COURTHOUSE DIV   FER

ON 02/28/01 AT 830 AM IN LONG BEACH COURTHOUSE DIV FER

CASE CALLED FOR PROGRESS REPORT
PARTIES: GARY J. FERRARI (JUDGE) IMELDA EVANCULLA   (CLERK)
                NONE (REP)   NONE (CP)
DEFENDANT IS NOT PRESENT IN COURT, AND NOT REPRESENTED BY COUNSEL

  PROBATION REVOKED
AS TO COUNT (01):
  DEFENDANT TO PAY FINE TO THE COURT CLERK
DMV ABSTRACT NOT REQUIRED
NEXT SCHEDULED EVENT:
  WARRANT ISSUED & CLDR CANCEL

03/02/01 BENCH WARRANT IN THE AMOUNT OF $50,000.00 BY ORDER OF JUDGE GARY J.
    FERRARI ISSUED. (03/02/01).

ON 03/30/01 AT 830 AM IN LONG BEACH COURTHOUSE DIV CRM

CASE CALLED FOR MISCELLANEOUS
PARTIES: NONE (JUDGE) JANICE WALTER (CLERK)
                NONE   (REP) NONE (DDA)
DEFENDANT IS PRESENT IN COURT, AND NOT REPRESENTED BY COUNSEL
  DEFENDANT APPEARS IN PRO PER
  WALKIN
NEXT SCHEDULED EVENT:

  03/30/01 830 AM BENCH WARRANT HEARING   DIST LONG BEACH COURTHOUSE DIV
    FER

ON 03/30/01 AT 830 AM IN LONG BEACH COURTHOUSE DIV FER

CASE CALLED FOR BENCH WARRANT HEARING
PARTIES: GARY J. FERRARI (JUDGE) IMELDA EVANCULLA   (CLERK)
                THERESE CLAUSSEN (REP)   NONE (CP)
DEFENDANT IS PRESENT IN COURT, AND NOT REPRESENTED BY COUNSEL
  DEFENDANT APPEARS IN PRO PER
PROBATION REINSTATED
  PROBATION IS CONTINUED ON THE SAME TERMS AND CONDITIONS WITH THE FOLLOWING
    MODIFICATIONS:
AS TO COUNT (01):
DMV ABSTRACT NOT REQUIRED
NEXT SCHEDULED EVENT:
  08/30/01 830 AM FINES/FEES   DIST LONG BEACH COURTHOUSE DIV FER

Pg 106

03/30/01 BENCH WARRANT IN THE AMOUNT OF $50,000.00   RECALLED. (03/30/01).

ON 08/30/01 AT 830 AM IN LONG BEACH COURTHOUSE DIV FER

CASE CALLED FOR FINES/FEES
PARTIES: TOMSON T ONG (JUDGE) IMELDA EVANCULLA (CLERK)
         THERESE CLAUSSEN   (REP) NONE (CP)
DEFENDANT IS PRESENT IN COURT, AND NOT REPRESENTED BY COUNSEL
  DEFENDANT APPEARS IN PRO PER
PAYMENT IN THE AMOUNT OF $135.00 PAID ON 08/30/01 RECEIPT # LBH452074007
  DEFT. TO PAY $200 RESTITUTION FINE TODAY
NEXT SCHEDULED EVENT:
  11/30/01 830 AM PROOF OF COMMUNITY SERVICE   DIST LONG BEACH COURTHOUSE
    DIV CLK

ON 11/30/01 AT 830 AM IN LONG BEACH COURTHOUSE DIV CRM

CASE CALLED FOR MISCELLANEOUS
PARTIES: NONE (JUDGE) NONE (CLERK)
         NONE   (REP) NONE (DDA)
DEFENDANT IS PRESENT IN COURT, AND NOT REPRESENTED BY COUNSEL
  WALK-IN FOR AM COURT
NEXT SCHEDULED EVENT:
  11/30/01 830 AM MISCELLANEOUS   DIST LONG BEACH COURTHOUSE DIV FER

ON 11/30/01 AT 830 AM IN LONG BEACH COURTHOUSE DIV FER

CASE CALLED FOR MISCELLANEOUS
PARTIES: GARY J. FERRARI (JUDGE) IMELDA EVANCULLA (CLERK)
         THERESE CLAUSSEN   (REP) PETER R. BREGMAN (CP)
DEFENDANT IS PRESENT IN COURT, AND NOT REPRESENTED BY COUNSEL
  DEFENDANT APPEARS IN PRO PER

NEXT SCHEDULED EVENT:
  03/29/02 830 AM PROOF OF COMMUNITY SERVICE   DIST LONG BEACH COURTHOUSE
    DIV CLK

ON 03/29/02 AT 800 AM IN LONG BEACH COURTHOUSE DIV CRM

CASE CALLED FOR MISCELLANEOUS
PARTIES: NONE (JUDGE) NANCY JAUREGUI (CLERK)
         NONE   (REP) NONE (DDA)
DEFENDANT IS PRESENT IN COURT, AND NOT REPRESENTED BY COUNSEL
  WALK-IN A.M.
NEXT SCHEDULED EVENT:
  03/29/02 830 AM MISCELLANEOUS   DIST LONG BEACH COURTHOUSE DIV FER

ON 03/29/02 AT 830 AM IN LONG BEACH COURTHOUSE DIV FER

CASE CALLED FOR MISCELLANEOUS

PARTIES: GARY J. FERRARI (JUDGE) TYRA BAHAM (CLERK)
              THERESE CLAUSSEN   (REP) SANDRA L. STOLPE (CP)
DEFENDANT IS PRESENT IN COURT, AND NOT REPRESENTED BY COUNSEL
  DEFENDANT APPEARS IN PRO PER
NEXT SCHEDULED EVENT:
  07/29/02   830 AM PROOF OF COMMUNITY SERVICE   DIST LONG BEACH COURTHOUSE
    DIV CLK

ON 07/29/02 AT 800 AM IN LONG BEACH COURTHOUSE DIV CRM

CASE CALLED FOR MISCELLANEOUS
PARTIES: NONE (JUDGE) NONE (CLERK)
              NONE   (REP) NONE (DDA)
DEFENDANT IS PRESENT IN COURT, AND NOT REPRESENTED BY COUNSEL
  WALK-IN AM JF
NEXT SCHEDULED EVENT:

  07/29/02   830 AM MISCELLANEOUS   DIST LONG BEACH COURTHOUSE DIV FER

ON 07/29/02 AT 830 AM IN LONG BEACH COURTHOUSE DIV FER

CASE CALLED FOR MISCELLANEOUS
PARTIES: GARY J. FERRARI (JUDGE) TYRA BAHAM (CLERK)
              THERESE CLAUSSEN   (REP) PETER R. BREGMAN (CP)
DEFENDANT IS PRESENT IN COURT, AND NOT REPRESENTED BY COUNSEL
  DEFENDANT APPEARS IN PRO PER
NEXT SCHEDULED EVENT:
  12/02/02   830 AM PROOF OF COMMUNITY SERVICE   DIST LONG BEACH COURTHOUSE
    DIV CLK

ON 12/02/02 AT 830 AM IN LONG BEACH COURTHOUSE DIV CRM

CASE CALLED FOR MISCELLANEOUS
PARTIES: NONE (JUDGE) NONE (CLERK)

              NONE   (REP) NONE (DDA)
DEFENDANT IS PRESENT IN COURT, AND NOT REPRESENTED BY COUNSEL
  WALK IN FOR AM COURT
NEXT SCHEDULED EVENT:
  12/02/02   830 AM MISCELLANEOUS   DIST LONG BEACH COURTHOUSE DIV FER

ON 12/02/02 AT 830 AM IN LONG BEACH COURTHOUSE DIV FER

CASE CALLED FOR MISCELLANEOUS
PARTIES: TOMSON T ONG (JUDGE) AMY URUBURU (CLERK)
              STEFANIE A. ZUMBO   (REP) STEVEN M. SHAW (CP)
DEFENDANT IS PRESENT IN COURT, AND NOT REPRESENTED BY COUNSEL
  DEFENDANT APPEARS IN PRO PER
NEXT SCHEDULED EVENT:
  02/03/03   830 AM PROOF OF COMMUNITY SERVICE   DIST LONG BEACH COURTHOUSE
    DIV CLK

ON 02/07/03 AT   800 AM :

   CASE SENT TO D/FERRARI RE:CASE MISSED COURT ES

ON 02/18/03 AT   800 AM   IN LONG BEACH COURTHOUSE DIV   CRM

CASE CALLED FOR MISCELLANEOUS
PARTIES: NONE (JUDGE)   NONE (CLERK)
                NONE   (REP) NONE (DDA)
DEFENDANT IS PRESENT IN COURT, AND NOT REPRESENTED BY COUNSEL
   WALK-IN
NEXT SCHEDULED EVENT:
   02/18/03   830 AM MISCELLANEOUS   DIST LONG BEACH COURTHOUSE DIV   SOJ

ON 02/18/03 AT   830 AM   IN LONG BEACH COURTHOUSE DIV   CRM

CASE CALLED FOR MISCELLANEOUS
PARTIES: NONE (JUDGE)   NONE (CLERK)
                NONE   (REP) NONE (DDA)
DEFENDANT IS NOT PRESENT IN COURT, AND NOT REPRESENTED BY COUNSEL
   CASE BACK FROM COURT
NEXT SCHEDULED EVENT:
PROCEEDING TERM & CLDR CANCEL

ON 02/18/03 AT   830 AM   IN LONG BEACH COURTHOUSE DIV   SOJ

CASE CALLED FOR MISCELLANEOUS
PARTIES: BRADFORD L. ANDREWS (JUDGE) TYRA BAHAM   (CLERK)
                 LOUISE COSTELLO (REP)   STEVEN M. SHAW (CP)
DEFENDANT IS PRESENT IN COURT, AND NOT REPRESENTED BY COUNSEL
   DEFENDANT APPEARS IN PRO PER
   PROBATION REVOKED
PROBATION REINSTATED

   PROBATION IS CONTINUED ON THE SAME TERMS AND CONDITIONS WITH THE FOLLOWING
     MODIFICATIONS:
AS TO COUNT (01):
   RESTITUION FINE PAID. COMMUNITY SERVICE COMPLETED
DMV ABSTRACT NOT REQUIRED
NEXT SCHEDULED EVENT:
   PROCEEDING TERM & CLDR CANCEL

ON 02/25/03 AT   800 AM :

NEXT SCHEDULED EVENT:
 UPON MOTION OF DEFENDANT
   03/20/03   830 AM MISCELLANEOUS   DIST LONG BEACH COURTHOUSE DIV   AND

ON 02/25/03 AT   830 AM :

   LETTER FROM CITY PROSECUTOR REQUESTING COURT DATE RECEIVED, RR

Pg 109

NEXT SCHEDULED EVENT:
 UPON MOTION OF DEFENDANT
  03/20/03   830 AM MISCELLANEOUS   DIST LONG BEACH COURTHOUSE DIV J/T
NEXT SCHEDULED EVENT:
  PROCEEDING TERM & CLDR CANCEL

ON 03/12/03 AT 830 AM IN LONG BEACH COURTHOUSE DIV J/T

CASE CALLED FOR MISCELLANEOUS
PARTIES: NONE (JUDGE) NONE (CLERK)
                NONE   (REP) NONE (DDA)
DEFENDANT IS NOT PRESENT IN COURT, AND NOT REPRESENTED BY COUNSEL
  CASE COMPLETED
NEXT SCHEDULED EVENT:
PROCEEDING TERM & CLDR CANCEL

ON 03/20/03 AT 800 AM :

  CLERK REQUESTED FILE/SENT TO D/J ES

ON 03/20/03 AT 830 AM :

  NO ACTION.
PROCEEDING TERM & CLDR CANCEL

04/15/16 ARREST DISPOSITION REPORT SENT VIA FILE TRANSFER TO DEPARTMENT OF
          JUSTICE

ON 04/27/16 AT 530 AM :

CASE FILE DESTROYED.

Pg 110

NO. 3LM00956   PAGE NO. 1
THE PEOPLE OF THE STATE OF CALIFORNIA   VS.   CURRENT DATE 06/08/18
DEFENDANT 01: ██████████████████
LAW ENFORCEMENT AGENCY EFFECTING ARREST: LONG BEACH POLICE DEPT.

BAIL: APPEARANCE   AMOUNT   DATE   RECEIPT OR   SURETY COMPANY   REGISTER
       DATE   OF BAIL   POSTED   BOND NO.   NUMBER

CASE FILED ON 02/25/03.
 COMPLAINT FILED, DECLARED OR SWORN TO CHARGING DEFENDANT WITH HAVING
COMMITTED, ON OR ABOUT 02/22/03 IN THE COUNTY OF LOS ANGELES, THE FOLLOWING
OFFENSE(S) OF:
    COUNT 01: 273.5(A) PC MISD
    COUNT 02: 242 PC MISD
NEXT SCHEDULED EVENT:
  02/25/03   830 AM ARRAIGNMENT   DIST LONG BEACH COURTHOUSE DIV D/V

ON 02/25/03 AT 830 AM IN LONG BEACH COURTHOUSE DIV D/V

CASE CALLED FOR ARRAIGNMENT
PARTIES: DEBORAH B. ANDREWS (JUDGE) E. DOMINGUEZ-MALAVE (CLERK)
              DIANA CARROLL (REP)   SHARON PANIAN (CP)
DEFENDANT IS PRESENT IN COURT, AND REPRESENTED BY PLESE 987.2 COURT APPOINTED
 COUNSEL
DEFENDANT ADVISED OF THE FOLLOWING RIGHTS ORALLY:
 DEFENDANT ARRAIGNED, AND ADVISED OF THE FOLLOWING RIGHTS: PLEAS
    AVAILABLE TO DEFENDANT; EXPLANATION OF NOLO CONTENDERE PLEA; TO
    THE AID OF AN ATTORNEY AT ALL STAGES OF THE PROCEEDINGS; TO A
    REASONABLE LENGTH OF TIME TO CONSULT AN ATTORNEY: THAT THE
    COURT WOULD APPOINT AN ATTORNEY FREE OF CHARGE IF DEFENDANT DOES
    NOT HAVE THE FINANCIAL MEANS TO RETAIN OWN; THAT UPON CONCLUSION
    OF THE CASE, THE COURT MAY ORDER A HEARING TO DETERMINE THE
    DEFENDANT'S THEN ABILITY TO PAY FOR ALL OR ANY PART OF THE COST
    OF APPOINTED COUNSEL, AND THAT DEFENDANT MAY BE ORDERED TO PAY
    ALL OR THAT PART OF SAID COSTS WITHIN DEFENDANT'S ABILITY TO
    PAY, RIGHT TO REPRESENT HIMSELF IN PRO PER AND ADVISED OF
    DISADVANTAGES OF SELF REPRESENTATION; NO SPECIAL TREATMENT BY
    COURT; PROSECUTOR EXPERIENCED ATTORNEY; CANNOT LATER CLAIM ERROR

    FOR INADEQUACY OF REPRESENTATION; THE DEFENDANT HAS BEEN ADVISED
    THAT THERE MAY BE DEFENSES THAT HE/SHE IS UNAWARE OF; TO PUBLIC
    TRIAL BY JURY OR COURT IN LONG BEACH; TO DISMISSAL IF NOT TRIED
    WITHIN 30 DAYS IF IN CUSTODY; WITHIN 45 DAYS IF NOT; TO THE AID
    OF THE COURT TO SUBPOENA AND PRODUCE WITNESSES ON OWN BEHALF; TO
    REASONABLE BAIL PENDING TRIAL; TO CONFRONT AND EXAMINE ADVERSE
    WITNESSES; TO EXERCISE PRIVILEGE AGAINST SELF INCRIMINATION AND
    REMAIN SILENT; INFORMED THAT BY ENTERING A PLEA OF GUILTY, THESE
    RIGHTS WOULD BE WAIVED; ADVISED RIGHT TO BE SENTENCED IN NOT
    LESS THAN 6 HOURS OR MORE THAN 5 DAYS UNLESS REFERRED TO THE
    PROBATION OFFICE; ADVISED MAXIMUM SENTENCE, UNLESS COURT
    INDICATED OTHERWISE, WOULD BE 1 YEAR COUNTY JAIL, $1,000 FINE OR
    BOTH; ADVISED MEANING OF PROBATION AND POSSIBLE OF LATER
    SENTENCE IF COURT DETERMINES VIOLATION; ADVISED IF ON PROBATION
    TO ANOTHER COURT THAT PLEA/CONVICTION MAY RESULT IN REVOCATION;

THE RIGHT TO HAVE A JUDGE REVIEW THE EVIDENCE TO DETERMINE IF
THERE IS PROBABLE CAUSE TO KEEP THE DEFENDANT IN CUSTODY UNTIL
TRIAL, THAT CONVICTION OF THE OFFENSE MAY HAVE THE CONSEQUENCES
OF DEPORTATION, EXCLUSION FROM ADMISSION TO THE UNITED STATES,
OR DENIAL OF NATURALIZATION
A COPY OF THE COMPLAINT AND THE ARREST REPORT GIVEN TO DEFENDANTS COUNSEL.
DEFENDANT WAIVES ARRAIGNMENT, READING OF COMPLAINT, AND STATEMENT OF
CONSTITUTIONAL AND STATUTORY RIGHTS.
DEFENDANT WAIVES FURTHER ARRAIGNMENT.
DEFENDANT ADVISED OF AND PERSONALLY AND EXPLICITLY WAIVES THE FOLLOWING RIGHTS:
TRIAL BY COURT AND TRIAL BY JURY
   CONFRONTATION AND CROSS-EXAMINATION OF WITNESSES;
   SUBPOENA OF WITNESSES INTO COURT TO TESTIFY IN YOUR DEFENSE;
   AGAINST SELF-INCRIMINATION;
DEFENDANT ADVISED OF THE FOLLOWING:
 THE NATURE OF THE CHARGES AGAINST HIM, THE ELEMENTS OF THE OFFENSE IN THE
   COMPLAINT, AND POSSIBLE DEFENSES TO SUCH CHARGES;
 THE POSSIBLE CONSEQUENCES OF A PLEA OF GUILTY OR NOLO CONTENDERE, INCLUDING

   THE MAXIMUM PENALTY AND ADMINISTRATIVE SANCTIONS AND THE POSSIBLE LEGAL
   EFFECTS AND MAXIMUM PENALTIES INCIDENT TO SUBSEQUENT CONVICTIONS FOR THE
   SAME OR SIMILAR OFFENSES;
 THE EFFECTS OF PROBATION;
 IF YOU ARE NOT A CITIZEN, YOU ARE HEREBY ADVISED THAT A CONVICTION OF THE
   OFFENSE FOR WHICH YOU HAVE BEEN CHARGED WILL HAVE THE CONSEQUENCES OF
   DEPORTATION, EXCLUSION FROM ADMISSION TO THE UNITED STATES, OR DENIAL OF
   NATURALIZATION PURSUANT TO THE LAWS OF THE UNITED STATES.
THE DEFENDANT WITH THE COURTS APPROVAL, PLEADS NOLO CONTENDERE TO COUNT 01 A
   VIOLATION OF SECTION 273.5(A) PC. THE COURT FINDS THE DEFENDANT GUILTY.
COUNT (01) : DISPOSITION: CONVICTED
DEFENDANT IS ADVISED OF HIS RIGHT TO A SPEEDY TRIAL AND WAIVES STATUTORY TIME
   FOR TRIAL.
COURT ACCEPTS PLEA
NEXT SCHEDULED EVENT:
   SENTENCING
   DEFENDANT WAIVES ARRAIGNMENT FOR JUDGMENT AND STATES THERE IS NO LEGAL CAUSE
   WHY SENTENCE SHOULD NOT BE PRONOUNCED. THE COURT ORDERED THE FOLLOWING
   JUDGMENT:
AS TO COUNT (01):
IMPOSITION OF SENTENCE SUSPENDED

DEFENDANT PLACED ON SUMMARY PROBATION
   FOR A PERIOD OF 003 YEARS UNDER THE FOLLOWING TERMS AND CONDITIONS:
   SERVE 004 DAYS IN LOS ANGELES COUNTY JAIL
      LESS CREDIT FOR 4 DAYS
   PLUS $100.00 ALCOHOL AND DRUG PROBLEM ASSESSMENT (23649 V.C.)
    $200.00 DOMESTIC VIOLENCE FUND(PURSUANT TO 1203.097 P.C.)
    $35.00 INSTALLMENT & ACCOUNTS RECEIVABLE FEE (PURSUANT TO 1205(D)PC)
   PERFORM 40 HOURS OF COMMUNITY SERVICE
   DEFENDANT SHALL PAY RESTITUTION IN THE AMOUNT OF $100.00 TO COURT THROUGH THE
      COURT
      TOTAL DUE: $435.00
   IN ADDITION:
   -NOT HARASS, MOLEST OR ANNOY VICTIM DOMESTIC VIOLENCE PROGRAM.
   -NOT OWN, USE OR POSSESS ANY DANGEROUS OR DEADLY WEAPONS,
    INCLUDING ANY FIREARMS, KNIVES OR OTHER CONCEALABLE WEAPONS.

  -COOPERATE WITH THE PUBLIC HEALTH OFFICER IN A PLAN FOR WITHIN
     48 HOURS AFTER RELEASE FROM CUSTODY, AND BE ENROLLED IN A
     DOMESTIC VIOLENCE PROGRAM WITHIN 21 DAYS THEREAFTER. DEFENDANT
     TO RETURN TO COURT ON 022504.
  -DEFENDANT SHALL REPORT TO THE PUBLIC HEALTH INVESTIGATOR
     ??

  OBEY ALL LAWS AND FURTHER ORDERS OF THE COURT.
  RELEASE ISSUED #AY003682.
  PROTECTIVE ORDER SIGNED, FILED, SERVED TO DEFENDANT IN COURT.
COUNT (01): DISPOSITION: CONVICTED
REMAINING COUNTS DISMISSED:
  COUNT (02): DISMISSAL IN FURTH OF JUSTICE PER 1385 PC
DMV ABSTRACT NOT REQUIRED
NEXT SCHEDULED EVENT:
  03/28/03   830 AM PROGRESS REPORT   DIST LONG BEACH COURTHOUSE DIV D/V
NEXT SCHEDULED EVENT:

  05/22/03   830 AM FINES/FEES   DIST LONG BEACH COURTHOUSE DIV D/V
NEXT SCHEDULED EVENT:
  02/25/04   830 AM PROOF OF DOMESTIC VIOL CLASS   DIST LONG BEACH COURTHOUSE
     DIV D/V

ON 02/26/03 AT 800 AM IN LONG BEACH COURTHOUSE DIV CRM

CASE CALLED FOR FINES/FEES
PARTIES: NONE (JUDGE) VERONICA GONZALES (CLERK)
              NONE   (REP) NONE (DDA)
DEFENDANT IS PRESENT IN COURT, AND NOT REPRESENTED BY COUNSEL
PAYMENT IN THE AMOUNT OF $200.00 PAID ON 02/26/03 RECEIPT # LBH482047003
  RECEIVED PARTIAL PAYMENT.
NEXT SCHEDULED EVENT:
  05/22/03   830 AM FINES/FEES   DIST LONG BEACH COURTHOUSE DIV CLK

ON 03/21/03 AT 800 AM :

  NOTIFICATION OF ENROLLMENT RECEIVED, RR

ON 03/28/03 AT 830 AM IN LONG BEACH COURTHOUSE DIV D/V

CASE CALLED FOR PROGRESS REPORT
PARTIES: DEBORAH B. ANDREWS (JUDGE) CHERRY GAINES (CLERK)
              DIANA CARROLL   (REP) SHARON PANIAN (CP)
DEFENDANT IS PRESENT IN COURT, AND NOT REPRESENTED BY COUNSEL
NEXT SCHEDULED EVENT:
FINES/FEES

ON 04/23/03 AT 800 AM IN LONG BEACH COURTHOUSE DIV CRM

CASE CALLED FOR MISCELLANEOUS
PARTIES: NONE (JUDGE) VERONICA GONZALES (CLERK)
              NONE   (REP) NONE (DDA)

Pg 113

CASE NO. 3LM00956   PAGE NO.   4
DEF NO. 01   DATE PRINTED 06/08/18

DEFENDANT IS PRESENT IN COURT, AND NOT REPRESENTED BY COUNSEL
 WALK-IN P.M. VICTIM WANTS TO LIFT P/O.
NEXT SCHEDULED EVENT:
 04/23/03   830 AM MISCELLANEOUS   DIST LONG BEACH COURTHOUSE DIV D/V

ON 04/23/03 AT 830 AM IN LONG BEACH COURTHOUSE DIV D/V

CASE CALLED FOR MISCELLANEOUS
PARTIES: DEBORAH B. ANDREWS (JUDGE) E. DOMINGUEZ-MALAVE (CLERK)
              DIANA CARROLL   (REP) CALVIN GEORGE (CP)
DEFENDANT IS PRESENT IN COURT, AND NOT REPRESENTED BY COUNSEL
 PROTECTIVE ORDER TERMINATED FORTHWITH
NEXT SCHEDULED EVENT:
FINES/FEES

ON 05/22/03 AT 830 AM IN LONG BEACH COURTHOUSE DIV D/V

CASE CALLED FOR FINES/FEES
PARTIES: DEBORAH B. ANDREWS (JUDGE) CHERRY GAINES (CLERK)
              DIANA CARROLL   (REP) CALVIN GEORGE (CP)
DEFENDANT IS PRESENT IN COURT, AND REPRESENTED BY ICDA 987.2 COURT APPOINTED
 COUNSEL
PAYMENT IN THE AMOUNT OF $120.00 PAID ON 05/22/03 RECEIPT # LBH241240015
NEXT SCHEDULED EVENT:
 08/06/03   830 AM PROGRESS REPORT   DIST LONG BEACH COURTHOUSE DIV D/V

ON 05/30/03 AT 800 AM :

  NOTIFICATION OF PROGRESS RECEIVED, RR

ON 08/06/03 AT 830 AM IN LONG BEACH COURTHOUSE DIV D/V

CASE CALLED FOR PROGRESS REPORT
PARTIES: DEBORAH B. ANDREWS (JUDGE) CHERRY GAINES (CLERK)
              DIANA CARROLL   (REP) CALVIN GEORGE (CP)
DEFENDANT IS PRESENT IN COURT, AND NOT REPRESENTED BY COUNSEL
 DEFENDANT APPEARS IN PRO PER
 DEFENDANT TO PAY $115 FORTHWITH.
NEXT SCHEDULED EVENT:
 11/06/03   830 AM PROGRESS REPORT   DIST LONG BEACH COURTHOUSE DIV D/V
NEXT SCHEDULED EVENT:
 08/06/03   900 AM FINES/FEES   DIST LONG BEACH COURTHOUSE DIV CLK

ON 08/06/03 AT 900 AM IN LONG BEACH COURTHOUSE DIV CLK

CASE CALLED FOR FINES/FEES
PARTIES: NONE (JUDGE) NONE (CLERK)
              NONE   (REP) NONE (DDA)
DEFENDANT IS PRESENT IN COURT, AND NOT REPRESENTED BY COUNSEL

Pg 114

PAYMENT IN THE AMOUNT OF $115.00 PAID ON 08/06/03 RECEIPT # LBH241240001
NEXT SCHEDULED EVENT:
PROGRESS REPORT

ON 11/06/03 AT 830 AM IN LONG BEACH COURTHOUSE DIV D/V

CASE CALLED FOR PROGRESS REPORT
PARTIES: DEBORAH B. ANDREWS (JUDGE) CHERRY GAINES (CLERK)
                 DIANA CARROLL   (REP) CALVIN GEORGE (CP)
DEFENDANT IS PRESENT IN COURT, AND NOT REPRESENTED BY COUNSEL
  DEFENDANT APPEARS IN PRO PER
NEXT SCHEDULED EVENT:
  02/06/04   830 AM PROGRESS REPORT   DIST LONG BEACH COURTHOUSE DIV S08

ON 02/06/04 AT 830 AM IN LONG BEACH COURTHOUSE DIV S08

CASE CALLED FOR PROGRESS REPORT
PARTIES: DEBORAH B. ANDREWS (JUDGE) CHERRY GAINES (CLERK)
                 DIANA CARROLL   (REP) CALVIN GEORGE (CP)
DEFENDANT IS PRESENT IN COURT, AND NOT REPRESENTED BY COUNSEL
  45 DVP DONE.
NEXT SCHEDULED EVENT:
  04/13/04   830 AM PROGRESS REPORT   DIST LONG BEACH COURTHOUSE DIV S08

ON 04/01/04 AT 800 AM :

  COURT REFERRAL RECOMMENDATION RECEIVED,
  CLIENT HAS COMPLETED THE DOMESTIC VIOLENCE
  PROGRAM ON 03-24-04, RB

ON 04/13/04 AT 830 AM IN LONG BEACH COURTHOUSE DIV S08

CASE CALLED FOR PROGRESS REPORT
PARTIES: DEBORAH B. ANDREWS (JUDGE) CHERRY GAINES (CLERK)
                 DIANA CARROLL   (REP) CALVIN GEORGE (CP)
DEFENDANT IS PRESENT IN COURT, AND NOT REPRESENTED BY COUNSEL
  DVP DONE AND PAID. CASE COMPLETED
NEXT SCHEDULED EVENT:
PROCEEDING TERM & CLDR CANCEL

08/10/07 ARREST DISPOSITION REPORT SENT VIA FILE TRANSFER TO DEPARTMENT OF
          JUSTICE

ON 10/10/14 AT 530 AM :

CASE FILE DESTROYED.

Pg 115

NO. MA049694   PAGE NO. 1
THE PEOPLE OF THE STATE OF CALIFORNIA   VS.   CURRENT DATE 06/08/18
DEFENDANT 01:   ████████████████████
LAW ENFORCEMENT AGENCY EFFECTING ARREST: LASD - PALMDALE STATION

BAIL: APPEARANCE   AMOUNT   DATE   RECEIPT OR SURETY COMPANY   REGISTER
      DATE   OF BAIL   POSTED   BOND NO.   NUMBER

CASE FILED ON 07/13/10.
 COMPLAINT FILED, DECLARED OR SWORN TO CHARGING DEFENDANT WITH HAVING
 COMMITTED, ON OR ABOUT 07/06/10 IN THE COUNTY OF LOS ANGELES, THE FOLLOWING
OFFENSE(S) OF:
   COUNT 01: 273.5(A) PC FEL
NEXT SCHEDULED EVENT:
 07/13/10   830 AM ARRAIGNMENT   DIST ANTELOPE VALLEY CTHOUSE DEPT A01

ON 07/13/10 AT 830 AM IN ANTELOPE VALLEY CTHOUSE DEPT A01

CASE CALLED FOR ARRAIGNMENT
PARTIES: COMMR. ROBERT A. MCSORLEY (JUDGE) NANCY COFFIELD (CLERK)
              VICTORIA SLATTERY (REP)   JEFFERY GOOTMAN (DDA)
DEFENDANT DEMANDS COUNSEL.
COURT REFERS DEFENDANT TO THE PUBLIC DEFENDER.
PUBLIC DEFENDER APPOINTED. MANUEL R. MARTINEZ - P.D.
DEFENDANT IS PRESENT IN COURT, AND REPRESENTED BY MANUEL R. MARTINEZ DEPUTY
  PUBLIC DEFENDER
DEFENDANT WAIVES ARRAIGNMENT, READING OF COMPLAINT, AND STATEMENT OF
  CONSTITUTIONAL AND STATUTORY RIGHTS.
DEFENDANT PLEADS NOT GUILTY TO COUNT 01, 273.5(A) PC.
  COURT ORDERS AND FINDINGS:
  -THE COURT ORDERS THE DEFENDANT TO APPEAR ON THE NEXT COURT DATE.
DEFENDANT DEMANDS DETERMINATION OF PROBABLE CAUSE FOR ARREST.
COURT FINDS THERE IS PROBABLE CAUSE FOR ARREST OF DEFENDANT.
  PROTECTIVE ORDER IS ISSUED THIS DATE PURSUANT TO PENAL CODE
  SECTION 136.2 AND IS SERVED ON THE DEFENDANT IN OPEN COURT.

  PROTECTED PERSON: AISHI RAFFERTY

  DEFENSE DENIES ALL SPECIAL ALLEGATIONS.
BAIL SET AT $50,000.
NO STATUTORY TIME WAIVED.
NEXT SCHEDULED EVENT:
07/23/10   830 AM PRELIMINARY HEARING   DIST ANTELOPE VALLEY CTHOUSE DEPT A02
DAY 08 OF 10

CUSTODY STATUS: REMANDED TO CUSTODY

ON 07/23/10 AT 830 AM IN ANTELOPE VALLEY CTHOUSE DEPT A02

  NUNC PRO TUNC ORDER PREPARED. IT APPEARING TO THE COURT THAT THE MINUTE ORDER
  IN THE ABOVE ENTITLED ACTION DOES NOT PROPERLY REFLECT THE COURT'S ORDER. SAID
  MINUTE ORDER IS AMENDED NUNC PRO TUNC AS OF THAT DATE. ALL OTHER ORDERS ARE
TO REMAIN IN FULL FORCE AND EFFECT. DETAILS LISTED AT END OF THIS MINUTE ORDER.
CASE CALLED FOR PRELIMINARY HEARING
PARTIES: BERNIE C. LAFORTEZA (JUDGE) CLAUDIA V. ANZORA (CLERK)
              SUSAN E. GONZALEZ (REP)   PAUL MOLL (DA)

DEFENDANT IS PRESENT IN COURT, AND REPRESENTED BY JOHN HENDERSON DEPUTY PUBLIC
   DEFENDER
ON PEOPLES MOTION, COURT ORDERS COMPLAINT DEEMED AMENDED TO ALLEGE COUNT 01 AS
   A MISDEMEANOR PURSUANT TO 17B (1-5) OF THE PENAL CODE AND COUNT SHALL PROCEED
   AS A MISDEMEANOR.
DEFENDANT ADVISED OF THE FOLLOWING RIGHTS ORALLY:
DEFENDANT ADVISED OF AND PERSONALLY AND EXPLICITLY WAIVES THE FOLLOWING RIGHTS:
TRIAL BY COURT AND TRIAL BY JURY
     CONFRONTATION AND CROSS-EXAMINATION OF WITNESSES;
     SUBPOENA OF WITNESSES INTO COURT TO TESTIFY IN YOUR DEFENSE;
     AGAINST SELF-INCRIMINATION;
DEFENDANT ADVISED OF THE FOLLOWING:
  THE NATURE OF THE CHARGES AGAINST HIM, THE ELEMENTS OF THE OFFENSE IN THE
     COMPLAINT, AND POSSIBLE DEFENSES TO SUCH CHARGES;
  THE POSSIBLE CONSEQUENCES OF A PLEA OF GUILTY OR NOLO CONTENDERE, INCLUDING
     THE MAXIMUM PENALTY AND ADMINISTRATIVE SANCTIONS AND THE POSSIBLE LEGAL
     EFFECTS AND MAXIMUM PENALTIES INCIDENT TO SUBSEQUENT CONVICTIONS FOR THE
     SAME OR SIMILAR OFFENSES;

  THE EFFECTS OF PROBATION;
  IF YOU ARE NOT A CITIZEN, YOU ARE HEREBY ADVISED THAT A CONVICTION OF THE
     OFFENSE FOR WHICH YOU HAVE BEEN CHARGED WILL HAVE THE CONSEQUENCES OF
     DEPORTATION, EXCLUSION FROM ADMISSION TO THE UNITED STATES, OR DENIAL OF
     NATURALIZATION PURSUANT TO THE LAWS OF THE UNITED STATES.
THE COURT FINDS THAT EACH SUCH WAIVER IS KNOWINGLY, UNDERSTANDINGLY, AND
   EXPLICITLY MADE; COUNSEL JOINS IN THE WAIVERS
THE DEFENDANT PERSONALLY WITHDRAWS PLEA OF NOT GUILTY TO COUNT 01 AND PLEADS
   NOLO CONTENDERE WITH THE APPROVAL OF THE COURT TO A VIOLATION OF SECTION
   273.5(A) PC IN COUNT 01.   THE COURT FINDS THE DEFENDANT GUILTY.
COUNT (01) : DISPOSITION: CONVICTED
COURT FINDS THAT THERE IS A FACTUAL BASIS FOR DEFENDANT'S PLEA, AND COURT
   ACCEPTS PLEA.
NEXT SCHEDULED EVENT:
   SENTENCING
   DEFENDANT WAIVES ARRAIGNMENT FOR JUDGMENT AND STATES THERE IS NO LEGAL CAUSE
   WHY SENTENCE SHOULD NOT BE PRONOUNCED. THE COURT ORDERED THE FOLLOWING
   JUDGMENT:
AS TO COUNT   (01):
IMPOSITION OF SENTENCE SUSPENDED
DEFENDANT PLACED ON SUMMARY PROBATION

   FOR A PERIOD OF 036 MONTHS UNDER THE FOLLOWING TERMS AND CONDITIONS:
   SERVE 120 DAYS IN LOS ANGELES COUNTY JAIL
      LESS CREDIT FOR 28 DAYS
       FORTHWITH
   PLUS $30.00 COURT SECURITY ASSESSMENT (PURSUANT TO 1465.8(A)(1) P.C.)
      $30.00 CRIMINAL CONVICTION ASSESSMENT (PURSUANT TO 70373 G.C.)
      $400.00 DOMESTIC VIOLENCE FUND(PURSUANT TO 1203.097 P.C.)
   COMMITMENT ISSUED
   DEFENDANT TO PAY FINE TO THE COURT CLERK
   DEFENDANT SHALL PAY A RESTITUTION FINE IN THE AMOUNT OF $100.00 TO THE COURT
      TOTAL DUE: $560.00
   IN ADDITION:
   -ENROLL IN AND COMPLETE A 52 WEEK DOMESTIC VIOLENCE PROGRAM AND
      SHOW PROOF OF ENROLLMENT TO THE CLERK'S OFFICE BY 7-25-11.
   -DO NOT USE OR THREATEN TO USE FORCE OR VIOLENCE ON ANY PERSON.

DO NOT ANNOY, HARASS OR MOLEST ANY PERSON OR WITNESS INVOLVED IN
THIS CASE, ESPECIALLY AISHI LIAM RAFFERTY.
-DO NOT ASSOCIATE WITH/STAY AWAY FROM AISHI LIAM RAFFERTY.
-OBEY THE PROTECTIVE ORDER ISSUED IN THIS OR ANY OTHER CASE.
-DEFENDANT IS SERVED WITH A COPY OF THE PROTECTIVE ORDER IN OPEN
COURT.
-OBEY ALL LAWS AND ORDERS OF THE COURT.
-DEFENDANT ACKNOWLEDGES TO THE COURT THAT THE DEFENDANT
UNDERSTANDS AND ACCEPTS ALL THE PROBATION CONDITIONS, AND
DEFENDANT AGREES TO ABIDE BY SAME.
DEFENDANT TO PAY $560.00 TO THE CLERK'S OFFICE BY 7/25/11.

****
DUE TO COMPUTER PROGRAMMING ERROR, THE NUNC PRO TUNC LANGUAGE
ABOVE SHOULD BE DISREGARDED.

****
COUNT (01): DISPOSITION: CONVICTED

DMV ABSTRACT NOT REQUIRED
NEXT SCHEDULED EVENT:
  11/22/10   830 AM   PROOF OF ENROLLMENT   DIST ANTELOPE VALLEY CTHOUSE DEPT
  CLK
NEXT SCHEDULED EVENT:
  04/19/11   830 AM   PROGRESS REPORT   DIST ANTELOPE VALLEY CTHOUSE DEPT A05
NEXT SCHEDULED EVENT:
  07/25/11   830 AM   FINES/FEES   DIST ANTELOPE VALLEY CTHOUSE DEPT CLK

CUSTODY STATUS: ON PROBATION/REMANDED

ON 11/22/10 AT 900 AM :

  PROOF OF ENROLLMENT FOR DOMESTIC VIOLENCE PROGRAM RECEIVED AND
  FILED   DJ
PROGRESS REPORT

ON 04/19/11 AT 830 AM IN ANTELOPE VALLEY CTHOUSE DEPT A05

CASE CALLED FOR PROGRESS REPORT
PARTIES: BERNIE C. LAFORTEZA (JUDGE)   CLAUDIA V. ANZORA (CLERK)
              PENNY HILL   (REP) DONNA LYNN RAPPAPORT (DA)
DEFENDANT IS PRESENT IN COURT, AND NOT REPRESENTED BY COUNSEL
  PROGRESS ON THE DOMESTIC VIOLENCE COUNSELING PROGRAM IS FILED
  THIS DATE.

  FURTHER PROGRESS IS DUE IN THIS DEPARTMENT ON 7-20-11.

  THE DATE OF 7-25-11 TO REMAIN.

  COURT ORDERS AND FINDINGS:
  -THE COURT ORDERS THE DEFENDANT TO APPEAR ON THE NEXT COURT DATE.
NEXT SCHEDULED EVENT:
  07/20/11   830 AM PROGRESS REPORT   DIST ANTELOPE VALLEY CTHOUSE DEPT A05

NEXT SCHEDULED EVENT:
  FINES/FEES

CUSTODY STATUS: ON PROBATION

ON 07/20/11 AT 830 AM IN ANTELOPE VALLEY CTHOUSE DEPT A05

CASE CALLED FOR PROGRESS REPORT
PARTIES: CARLOS P. BAKER, JR. (JUDGE) CLAUDIA V. ANZORA (CLERK)
            FLOR ABADILLA   (REP) DONNA LYNN RAPPAPORT (DA)
DEFENDANT IS PRESENT IN COURT, AND NOT REPRESENTED BY COUNSEL
PAYMENT IN THE AMOUNT OF $560.00 PAID ON 07/20/11 RECEIPT # ATP500578001
  PROGRESS ON THE DOMESTIC VIOLENCE COUNSELING PROGRAM IS FILED
  THIS DATE.

  FURTHER PROGRESS ON THE PROGRAM IS DUE IN DEPARTMENT A5 ON
  10-18-11.

  THE DATE OF 7-25-11 IS VACATED.
  COURT ORDERS AND FINDINGS:
  -THE COURT ORDERS THE DEFENDANT TO APPEAR ON THE NEXT COURT DATE.
NEXT SCHEDULED EVENT:
  10/18/11 830 AM PROGRESS REPORT   DIST ANTELOPE VALLEY CTHOUSE DEPT A05

CUSTODY STATUS: ON PROBATION

ON 10/18/11 AT 830 AM IN ANTELOPE VALLEY CTHOUSE DEPT A05

CASE CALLED FOR PROGRESS REPORT
PARTIES: BERNIE C. LAFORTEZA (JUDGE) CLAUDIA V. ANZORA   (CLERK)
            SHARON FOX (REP)   RENA M. DURRANT (DA)
THE DEFENDANT FAILS TO APPEAR, WITHOUT SUFFICIENT EXCUSE AND NOT REPRESENTED BY
  COUNSEL
  PROBATION REVOKED
AS TO COUNT (01):
DMV ABSTRACT NOT REQUIRED
NEXT SCHEDULED EVENT:

  BENCH/WARRANT TO ISSUE

10/18/11 BENCH WARRANT IN THE AMOUNT OF $40,000.00 BY ORDER OF JUDGE BERNIE C.
  LAFORTEZA ISSUED. (10/18/11).

ON 10/20/11 AT 830 AM IN ANTELOPE VALLEY CTHOUSE DEPT A02

CASE CALLED FOR POSSIBLE VIOL. OF PROBATION
PARTIES: AKEMI ARAKAKI (JUDGE) CHERIE PINA   (CLERK)
            KATHRYN HOWELL (REP)   NONE ()
DEFENDANT IS PRESENT IN COURT, AND NOT REPRESENTED BY COUNSEL
PROBATION REINSTATED
  PROBATION IS CONTINUED ON THE SAME TERMS AND CONDITIONS WITH THE FOLLOWING
    MODIFICATIONS:
AS TO COUNT (01):
  COURT ORDERS AND FINDINGS:
  ORIGINAL TERMS AND CONDITIONS OF PROBATION TO REMAIN IN FULL
    FORCE AND EFFECT.

Pg 119

CASE NO. MA049694   PAGE NO.   5
DEF NO.   01   DATE PRINTED 06/08/18

    THE COURT ORDERS THE DEFENDANT TO APPEAR ON THE NEXT COURT DATE.
    DEFENDANT IS IN COURT AS A BENCH WARRANT WALK IN.

    THE COURT ACCEPTS PROGRESS IN THE DOMESTIC VIOLENCE COUNSELING
    PROGRAM, FURTHER PROGRESS/COMPLETION SET FOR 2-24-12.

    TCIS ENTERED BY K. ROBBINS.

DMV ABSTRACT NOT REQUIRED
NEXT SCHEDULED EVENT:
    02/24/12   830 AM PROOF OF DOMESTIC VIOL CLASS   DIST ANTELOPE VALLEY
      CTHOUSE DEPT A05

10/20/11 BENCH WARRANT IN THE AMOUNT OF $40,000.00   RECALLED. (10/20/11).

CUSTODY STATUS: ON PROBATION

ON 02/24/12 AT   830 AM IN ANTELOPE VALLEY CTHOUSE DEPT A05

CASE CALLED FOR PROOF OF DOMESTIC VIOL CLASS
PARTIES: AKEMI ARAKAKI (JUDGE) CHERIE PINA (CLERK)
                KATHRYN HOWELL   (REP) MARK A. ██████████ (DA)
DEFENDANT IS PRESENT IN COURT, AND NOT REPRESENTED BY COUNSEL
    DEFENDANT APPEARS IN PRO PER
    DEFENDANT SHOWS PROOF OF COMPLETION OF THE 52 WEEK DOMESTIC
    VIOLENCE COUNSELING PROGRAM.

    THE COURT FINDS DEFENDANT HAS FULFILLED ALL OBLIGATIONS.
    COURT ORDERS AND FINDINGS:
    -THE COURT ORDERS THE DEFENDANT TO APPEAR ON THE NEXT COURT DATE.
NEXT SCHEDULED EVENT:
PROBATION IN EFFECT

CUSTODY STATUS: ON PROBATION.

Pg 120

SECTION 4

Support Letters of Friends and Relative of
Petitioner and Beneficiary

Pg 121

June 15, 2018

To whom it may concern,

My name is Skyler Dorsett and I am a US citizen. I have been friends with
███████ █████ for 29 years. We were childhood friends who moved out from
Wisconsin to California together in our early 20's and have always maintained a close
friendship.

Matt met ██████████████ on Facebook just over a year ago on a group page
they were both a part of. They realized how much they had in common and became
fast friends, talking to each other every day. It was clear to my wife and me from early
on that they had a special connection. I have never, in all my years knowing Matt, seen
him this excited about anyone before. It's been wonderful to see Matt happy and
connected. Matt speaks of ████████ children with fondness and proudly shares
pictures of them as if they were his own.

Matt and ████████ made plans for her to come out and visit him in California in
August of last year and I was with him the night he found out that she would be unable
to make the trip. It was obvious how devastated they both were to be unable to meet in
person, but they continued talking daily until he was able to visit her and meet her family
in Botswana in February. This was when he asked her to marry him. Their fondness
for eachother is obvious and they interact every day, showing so much care, concern
and respect for each other.

To whom it May Concern,

We are writing to let you know that we are aware of our son Matthew's relationship with Tshepo Tawana. We support this relationship as we realize they have come to know and care for each other in a special way. His feelings for her are evident and they are committed to having a life together as they seek the best way. We look forward to meeting Tshepo and being supportive of them as a couple.

Sincerely,

Bill and Jan Shimer
N 3675 OAK HILL St
DELAVAN, WISCONSIN
53115

6/12/18

Pg 123

Matt ████ is one of my dearest friends. His loyalty, compassion, and integrity are unsurpassable. I am thrilled that Matt and ████ found each other and I wholeheartedly support their relationship. My wife and I look forward to the day we get to meet her in person.

Sincerely,

Skyer Dorsett

Skyer Dorsett

4447 Tulane Ave.

Long Beach, Ca 90808

www.ingramcontent.com/pod-product-compliance
Lightning Source LLC
Chambersburg PA
CBHW051756200326
41597CB00025B/4583